GOOD NEWS
for
GREAT DAYS

O.S. HAWKINS

Published by Annuity Board of the Southern Baptist Convention, Dallas, TX

Dewey Decimal Classification: 252.6 – dc21
Subject Heading: RELIGIOUS HOLIDAYS – SERMONS

Unless otherwise noted, Scripture quotations are from The Believer's Study
Bible, The Holy Bible, New King James version, copyright 1991, by the
Criswell Center for Biblical Studies.

Library of Congress Cataloging-in-Publication Data
Hawkins, O.S.
          Good News for Great Days / O.S. Hawkins
                    p. cm.
          Includes bibliographical references (p.).
          ISBN 0-9671584-3-5
          Library of Congress Card Catalog Number: 96-15883

ANNUITY BOARD
OF THE SOUTHERN
BAPTIST CONVENTION

Dedicated to:

L. D. Lusk

Through the years he has been a constant source of encouragement and support in the ministry I have received from the Lord. I wish every pastor, everywhere, could have by his side such a faithful, loving and dedicated layman and partner in ministry.

࿇

Contents

Foreword

On a personal note:

If you serve in a Southern Baptist church these paragraphs are unapologetically for you and they could be some of the most important paragraphs you will read. Although you will never "retire" from ministry, there will come a day when you will retire from vocational church service. We want that to be a great day for you. And it can be, if you are prepared.

King Solomon admonished us to "Go to the ant...consider her ways and be wise, which, having no captain, overseer or ruler, provides her supplies in the summer, and gathers her food in the harvest" (Prov. 6:6-8). If an ant is smart enough to put aside resources to meet the needs of an uncertain future, how much more should we? We are grieved for those who reach the end of a lifetime of ministry with little or no retirement funds in their declining years. For some of them it would have only taken some wise planning in their early years.

It is important to get started early in retirement planning. There is a thing called compound interest, which is extremely powerful. Let me illustrate. For example, assuming an 8% annual return, if a 25-year-old minister put $50 per month in his retirement account it would be worth $174,550 at age 65. If the same person waited until just the age of 35 to begin saving for retirement with the same $50 per month, it would be worth $74,520 at age 65, a difference of $100,000. It is very important to start early, but it is also important to start wherever you are along the way to retirement.

The beautiful and beneficial part of being in the Annuity Board program is the protection section. Did you know that if you or your church contribute only a few dollars per month to your retirement account, you automatically receive at no cost a survivor's benefit worth up to $100,000 to whomever you designate as your beneficiary? You also receive up to a $500 per month disability. This is a safety net every church should provide for their ministers.

We at the Annuity Board want to be a Life⊡Partner™ with you throughout your entire ministry. This is the driving reason behind new products which will give you additional opportunities to save for retirement, or whatever your saving needs. Soon you will be able to invest in personal savings programs and IRAs in addition to your 403(b) retirement account.

Yes, isn't it time for you to "go to the ant…and be wise?" For more information about these new personal investing products, matching contributions from your state conventions, protection benefits at no cost, housing allowance in retirement, our mission church assistance fund, our relief ministries or any of our other services visit us on the World Wide Web at *www.absbc.org* or better yet call us at **1-800-262-0511** and speak personally to one of our Customer Relations specialists.

O.S. Hawkins

New Year's Day:
Crossing over...into a new year

Deuteronomy 11:10-24

New Year's Day always brings an opportunity for a new beginning. For the children of Israel it had been a long journey. Moses had led them all the way from Egypt, through the Red Sea, to Kadesh Barnea, through the wilderness, and now they were encamped on the eastern bank of Jordan overlooking the promised land. The Book of Deuteronomy in the Old Testament records the sermons Moses preached to his people before he went up on Mount Nebo, viewed the promised land and died. In the aftermath of his death the children of Israel went on into the promised land and possessed it. Along the wilderness route there were often times when there were those who wrung their hands and doubted that they could go on and wished they were back in Egypt. Moses continued to remind them that God "brought us out from there that He might bring us in, to give us the land of which He had swore to our fathers" (Deut. 6:23).

Thus, before the blessing of the promised land became a reality for his faithful followers, Moses challenges them with these words from Deut. 11:10-24. He reminds them as they cross over to their promised possession that they do so with God's provision, God's presence, God's promise and God's protection.

As we stand at the brink of a new year our hearts are filled with anticipation and challenge. Only God knows what the future holds but the possibilities are limitless. As we cross over into a new year we do so with the same challenges Moses gave his people so long ago. As we cross over into a new year we're reminded of:

God's provision

 But the land you cross over to possess is a land of hills and valleys, which drinks water from the rain of heaven (Deut. 11:11).

What is Moses saying to Israel here? Better yet, what is God saying to us through their experience? He will meet our needs! He is our source. Like the land of Israel, our land will "drink water from the rain of heaven." How many times have we seen this across the years…when it looked like hope was almost gone? In those times when we began to feel our source was running out, "God would rain from heaven the blessing upon us." We cross over into a new year reminded that He is our source.

Moses reminded the people that the land that they were about to possess was a land of "hills and valleys." God never promised us the way would always be easy. It is not a mountaintop experience all the time. Sometimes we too, like the

Israelites, walk through the valley. And then, there are those times when we come face to face with a mountain along the journey which humanly speaking looks impossible to climb.

Yes, it is a land of "hills and valleys." Anyone who's ever traveled in the promised land knows the reality of this visual expression. There are deep valleys. I've walked through the Kidron Valley and through Wadi Kelt. There are high mountains like Mount Hermon and Masada. There are desert places in the Judean wilderness and then there's the beautiful oasis of Jericho. It did not take the children of Israel long to discover that it was indeed a land of hills and valleys. They began their conquest of the promised land with the great victory at Jericho only to descend into the valley of defeat at Ai in the days that came afterwards.

The same is true for us along our own journeys. Ours too is a journey through "hills and valleys." Thank God for the hills, the mountains. Often in the valleys we forget about the mountains. And, unfortunately, often when we're on the mountain we forget about the valleys. Both are important! If there were no valleys there would be no mountain tops. We never learn spiritual lessons on the mountain. They are always learned in the valley where we're trusting, depending on the living God to get us through. Mountains are there to enlarge our vision, to let us see our potential, to give us a spirit of conquest. But in the valleys, that's where we become more like our Lord. We would not choose the valleys. But His ways are not our ways. He is in fact the God of the mountains. He is also the God of the valleys. Do you remember what Elijah said to Ahab when Ben-Hadad, the cruelest general to ever march an army, besieged the city of Samaria? Elijah said, "... 'Because the Syrians have said, the Lord is God of the hills but He is not God of the valleys,' therefore, I will deliver all this great multitude into your hand, and you shall know that I am the Lord" (I Kin. 20:28). Yes, it is a land of hills and valleys.

But look closely at Deut. 11:11. Note that we take with us into a new year the promise of God's provision. "It is a land that drinks rain from heaven." That is, He provides for us supernaturally.

For the children of Israel the land of Israel was quite a contrast from the past years of Egypt. Moses reminds them that the land which they were about to possess was "not like the land of Egypt ... where you sowed your seed and watered it by foot" (Deut. 11:10). What was the difference? The land of Egypt depended on human resources. There was not much rain. The Nile was their source and it overflowed once a year. Therefore hard work was involved. By hand and by foot they dug trenches, canals to irrigate the land. In Egypt it was all done by human effort. Work, work, work was the motto. In Egypt there was no need for God. Water was stored by artificial means and fields were irrigated by human sweat and toil. Egypt did not depend on God like Canaan did.

There are a lot of churches today that operate like the children of Israel in Egypt. That is, they have it all calculated with human ingenuity. They dig their own trenches. There's no real need for God. They go right on operating without Him, with their own initiatives, plans and promotions. They do not do anything that cannot be explained by human means. Most everything happens by human effort and ingenuity.

But note the contrast of the promised land. It "drinks water from the rain of heaven." Canaan was and is totally dependent on God. Rain was His gift. In fact, this land has always been solely dependent upon His provisions. Perhaps that's why He chose this land and those people to train His church. I Cor. 10:6 reminds us that everything that happened to the children of Israel did so as an example to us in this dispensation of grace. How beautiful to know that He proves this with both autumn and spring rains (Deut 11:14). He sends the early rain for seed time and the latter rain at harvest. Both are important for growing a good crop.

As we cross over into a new year we do so with the assurance that the same God who sends us the autumn rains of the past will send us the spring rains in the future. It may be a land of hills and valleys but it is a land that "drinks rain from heaven." As we cross over we're dependent on the supernatural provision of God. God is our source and he has a way of using us to accomplish his purpose. As we cross over into a new year we do so with God's provision. We also cross over with:

God's presence

 A land which the Lord your God cares; the eyes of the Lord your God are always on it, from the beginning of the year to the very end of the year (Deut. 11:12).

Remember, the Apostle Paul reminds us that everything that happened to the children of Israel happened as examples for us (I Cor. 10:6). There were some who said to Moses that they doubted they could accomplish the task of taking the promised land. After all, the land was filled with giants and walled cities. But they had forgotten that they crossed over with God's provision and God's presence. It was "a land which the Lord your God cares; the eyes of the Lord your God are always on it, from the beginning of the year to the very end of the year" (Deut. 11:11). The year upon which we embark is a year that God cares for. He purposed it. He planned it. He knows the way through the wilderness and all we have to do is follow.

Some of the sweetest words in Deuteronomy 11:12 are often overlooked. Moses refers to the God of Israel as "your" God. He is a personal Lord and Savior. We are in covenant with Him. We are His and He is ours. Moses reminds his people that this is true "from the beginning of the year to the very end of the year." As we cross over into a new year we're reminded that God is watching us, that His eyes are upon us.

New Year's Day brings a fresh vision of new opportunities. What a blessing to cross over into a new year with the very presence of God Himself. The eyes of the Lord are upon us! He is watching the dear mother who faces the year raising children without a husband. He is watching the dad who's under tremendous pressure to provide. He's watching the teenager with all the pressures of adolescence. He's watching each of us. Yes, "For the eyes of the Lord run to and fro throughout the whole earth, to show Himself strong on behalf of those whose heart is loyal to Him" (II Chr. 16:8-10). Like the children of Israel, He did not bring us out except to take us in. We go into a new year with God's provision and God's presence. We also go with:

God's promise

 And it shall be that if you earnestly obey My commandments which I command you today, to love the Lord your God and serve Him with all your heart and with all your soul,

Then I will give you the rain for your land in its season, the early rain and the latter rain, that you may gather in your grain, your new wine, and your oil.

And I will send grass in your fields for your livestock, that you may eat and be filled (Deut. 11: 13-15).

What was Moses saying to Israel? Better yet, what is God saying to us? Remember that all these things happened to the children of Israel who are examples to us in this dispensation of grace. The single most important thing we can do as we cross over into a new year is to love the Lord our God and to serve Him with all our hearts.

Note that this promise is conditional. Verse 13 begins with "if" and verse 14 begins with "then." Thus, this promise is not for everyone. It is for whom? Those who love the Lord their God and serve Him with all their heart and soul. Think about it. What could be more simple? Israel only had to walk in obedience to God's word and to love Him. All that kept them from the blessing of God was disobedience. It is the same with us. I often wonder what would happen to the church of Jesus Christ if all of the members began to truly love the Lord with all their heart and serve Him with all their soul.

Here we find the Israelites' primary purpose. It was to love

God! Everything in life has a primary purpose. The primary purpose of a pen is to write. I would rather have a cheap plastic pen that worked than an expensive one that didn't. The primary purpose of an automobile is to transport us from place to place. I would rather have a 10-year-old automobile that always started than a shiny new one that did not work. When something ceases to fulfill its primary purpose it becomes useless. We've all seen wrecking yards with hundreds of cars lined up side by side that once were valuable. Could it be that so many Christians are defeated because so few are fulfilling their primary purpose? All of God's commandments are pure but the Lord Jesus said one was the greatest. It was to love God with all of our hearts (Matt. 22:37). I might add that the reason we break most of the other commandments is because we do not obey this great commandment. Men and women would not defile their bodies in adultery or fornication if they loved God with all their hearts. No wonder Moses spoke this stern warning related to God's promise in Deuteronomy 11:13-14.

Moses reminded the children of Israel, and us, what is of utmost importance — loving God. We're to love God first and love man second. This is the fallacy of humanism that infiltrates so much of our culture. It says that the way to love God is to love man first. The Bible says the only way I can truly love others on the highest level of love is to love God supremely.

As we enter a new year we do so with God's promise. What is our primary purpose? It is to love Him. It is to love God and serve Him with all of our hearts and souls.

Thus, we cross over into a new year with God's provision. We are reminded that He is our source. We cross over with

God's presence. We are reminded that His eyes are upon us from the beginning of the year to the end of the year. We cross over with God's promise. If we love Him and serve Him with all of our hearts then His blessing will be upon us. Finally, we cross over to a new year.

God's protection

 Take heed to yourselves, lest your heart be deceived, and you turn aside and serve other gods and worship them,

Lest the Lord's anger be aroused against you, and He shut up the heavens so that there be no rain, and the land yield no produce, and you perish quickly from the good land which the Lord is giving you.

Therefore you shall lay up these words of mine in your heart and in your soul, and bind them as a sign on your hand, and they shall be as frontlets between your eyes.

You shall teach them to your children, speaking of them when you sit in your house, when you walk by the way, when you lie down, and when you rise up.

And you shall write them on the doorposts of your house and on your gates,

That your days and the days of your children may be multiplied in the land of which the Lord swore to your fathers to give them, like the days of the heavens above the earth.

*For if you carefully keep all these commandments
which I command you to do — to love the Lord your
God, to walk in all His ways, and to hold fast to Him —*

*Then the Lord will drive out all these nations from
before you, and you will dispossess greater and
mightier nations than yourselves.*

*Every place on which the sole of your foot treads
shall be yours: from the wilderness and Lebanon,
from the river, the River Euphrates, even to the
Western Sea, shall be your territory (Deut. 11:16-24).*

What is Moses saying to Israel? Better yet, what is God saying to us since what happened to them was simply an example for us? He is reminding us that the Lord will go before us and drive out our enemies. His protection carries with it a warning. "Take heed to yourselves, lest your heart be deceived, and you turn aside and serve other gods and worship them, lest the Lord's anger be aroused against you, and He shut up the heavens so that there be no rain, and the land yield no produce, and you perish quickly from the good land which the Lord is giving you" (Deut. 11:16-17). Again, note the repetition of the importance of loving our God. "For if you carefully keep all these commandments which I command you to do—to love the Lord your God, to walk in all His ways and to hold fast to Him" (Deut. 11:22). For any of us who wonder why we may be living outside the provision and protection of God the reason might be found in this verse.

Moses is tying his people to the word of God. Hear him as he challenges his people —" You shall lay up these words of mine in your heart and in your soul, and bind them as a sign on your hand, and they shall be frontlets between your eyes. You shall teach them to your children, speaking of them when you sit in your house, when you walk by the way, when you lie down and when you rise up" (Deut. 11:18-19). Moses knew the only way his people could love the Lord with all their heart was to saturate themselves with a conscious awareness of His word. As we cross over into a new year we do so with God's protection. Moses goes on to tell them that "Then the Lord will drive out all these nations from before you, and you will dispossess greater and mightier nations than yourselves. Every place on which the sole of your foot treads shall be yours: from the wilderness and Lebanon, from the river, the River Euphrates, even to the Western Sea, shall be your territory. No man shall be able to stand against you" (Deut. 11:23-25).

Yes, it was a long continuous journey for the children of Israel through the decades of wilderness wanderings. Moses led them all the way. And thus he comes to the end of his own life and says, "The land which you cross over to possess is a land of hills and valleys, which drinks water from the rain of heaven, a land which the Lord your God cares; the eyes of the Lord your God are always on it, from the beginning of the year to the very end of the year" (Deut. 11:11-12). As we cross over to this new year Moses stands to remind us that as we go, we too will need God's provision. To depend on human effort is sheer folly. We will need God's presence. There will be times when we, like the children of Israel, wonder where God is. But His eyes are upon us. We cross over with God's promise. There may be times that this is all we have to hold. And, we go with His protection.

There may be times when we'll be without help or hope unless God supernaturally intervenes.

We, too, have been on a journey. Now we are crossover people ourselves. We are crossing over into a new year with new opportunities and new beginnings. Yes, He brought us out from there that He might bring us in to a land of blessing. As we enter a new year let us, like those who've gone before, love God…walk in His ways…and hold fast to Him.

Sanctity of Life Day:
Choose life

Deuteronomy 30:19

"Legal personhood does not exist prenatally"...so declared the United States Supreme Court in the now infamous Roe v. Wade decision handed down on January 22, 1973. Since that day, millions of babies have been legally aborted in our nation. In its aftermath has not only come the elimination of millions of lives, but tragic trauma to millions of mothers. "Legal personhood does not exist prenatally." Tell that to the lady who wrote me these words:

"Nearing forty years of age and after four children, I found myself pregnant. My husband suggested abortion. I knew in my heart it was wrong, I have suffered supreme remorse ever since. Our home has one empty bedroom — a constant reminder! The doctors could control my problem, but nobody can control my hurt and loss of a very precious life that God Himself created. I carry this around now and for the rest of my life this awful memory, the hurt is all mine.

You can tell young women who may be considering abortion that a woman never forgets her baby. The memory lives on and on."

On July 1, 1976, the week of our National Bicentennial Celebration, the Supreme Court expanded its 1973 decision by declaring that abortions may be performed on minor daughters without the knowledge of their parents. It is a strange nation in which we are living where an adolescent cannot get an aspirin in a school infirmary without parental permission, but can have an abortion without such! The 1976 decision also expanded the 1973 decision to allow women to obtain an abortion without the knowledge or consent of the baby's father. While a father must pay child support in other cases (and rightly so), he is often left with no say as to whether his own child comes into the world or not.

Perhaps no other moral or social issue is as many faceted as is the abortion debate. Any serious discussion of the matter will eventually come down to one central issue — when does life begin? This is "the big question." Some say life begins at birth. They contend that until the baby is out of the womb it is not to be considered a human being, simply a "fetus." Others say life begins when the fetus has grown and developed enough to live outside the womb if need be. Consequently, this particular school of thought would say life begins at five to six months. Others say life begins when the baby has a measured brain wave. The argument here is that the secession of a brain wave marks the end of human life, and thus it naturally stands to reason that the beginning of the brain wave would be the beginning of human life. A brain wave can be measured at approximately six weeks after conception. Still others claim that life begins when the baby develops a measured heart beat. Such advocates thus place the beginning of life at approximately three to four weeks after conception. And, others would say that life begins at conception. That is, when the male cell and the female cell unite, thus beginning the life process.

When does life begin? Consider for a moment the argument from science. The nucleus of a human cell is composed of 46 chromosomes. Twenty-three are furnished by the father, and 23 are furnished by the mother. The abortionists argue that during the embryonic stage of development and in the early stages of fetal development, the baby could not survive apart from the mother's body. Thus, their argument is that it is moral to eliminate the fetus if so desired. But the truth is, the same baby could not survive apart from the mother's care after it is born at nine months either. To follow this erroneous concept to its conclusion would be to go ahead and eliminate the baby even after birth.

It is a fact of biological science that the only cell that the mother contributes to the baby is the first one (23 chromosomes) when it meets the father's cell and they combine. At this point conception takes place, and a new person is formed. In the cell structure, the baby is as much a part of the father as the mother. Obviously, during gestation the baby is nourished through the umbilical cord by the mother. But it should be noted that only the baby is nourished. The same baby, after birth, is also dependent upon being nourished by the mother outside the womb. After conception, the child receives no new or additional life from the mother. It is not a part of her body that can be removed like a wart or a tumor. It is an individual person.

It is amazing how abortion activists refrain from using the

term "baby" for the unborn and instead cling to the less inti-
mate word, "fetus." It is as though this gives more of an appearance that the baby is simply a part of the mother's anatomy like
a gall bladder or an appendix. It sounds so much better to say
the fetus was extracted than to say the baby was killed. The pro-
abortion activist might be interested to know that the word
"fetus" is a Latin word. What does it mean in Latin? It is the
word for "child." Life is a continual process, and each of us is
a part of it. Some of us are newly conceived. Others are developing in the womb. Some are just born. Others are toddlers in
the nursery. Some have completed the first day of school.
Others are adolescents. Some are adults. Others are elderly. But
we are all in a stage of gradual development. Man is no more
or less a person at any stage of this development.

When does life begin? Consider for a moment the argument of Scripture. Just because many influenced by New
Age persuasions have placed the Bible on the shelf as a worn
out book of antiquity, does not mean it is. Millions of people
still hold its truths near and dear to their hearts. Its words and
laws have been the foundation blocks for every decent democ-
racy and republic in world history We believe it is revealed
truth and our ultimate standard. Jesus stepped into manhood,
not at His birth at Bethlehem, but at His conception at
Nazareth. The Scripture records, "An angel of the Lord
appeared to Joseph in a dream and said, 'Do not be afraid to
take to you Mary as your wife, for that which is conceived in
her is of the Holy Spirit'" (Matt. 1:20). To Mary, the angel
announced, "And behold, you will conceive in your womb and
bring forth a son, and shall call His name Jesus" (Luke 1:31).

As many are aware, the New Testament was written in the Greek language. It was the universal written language of the first-century world.

The Greeks have more than one word for our English word, "child." The most common word, found over ninety-eight times in the Greek New Testament is the word "teknon." The word speaks of a child as viewed in relation to a parent. However, there is an interesting word that is found only eight times in the Greek New Testament which throws much light upon what the Bible teaches regarding the unborn. It is the Greek word, "brephos." Note its usage in the following verses:

> *This man dealt treacherously with our people, and oppressed our forefathers, making them expose their babies (*brephos)*, so that they might not live (Acts 7:19).*

> *Then they also brought infants (*brephos) *to Him that He might touch them; but when the disciples saw it, they rebuked them (Luke 18:15).*

> *And that from childhood (*brephos) *you have known the Holy Scriptures, which are able to make you wise for sal-vation through faith which is in Christ Jesus (II Tim. 3:15).*

> *As newborn babes (*brephos)*, desire the pure milk of the word, that you may grow thereby (I Pet. 2:2).*

> *And this will be the sign to you: You will find a Babe (*brephos) *wrapped in swaddling cloths, lying in a manger (Luke 2:12).*

> *And they came with haste and found Mary and*

> *Joseph, and the Babe* (brephos) *lying in a manger (Luke 2:16).*

In all the above verses the word *brephos* describes a baby who has already been born. One who is outside the womb! That is, a real live human being. But there are two other verses in Scripture in which the same Greek word *(brephos)* is used. One is in Luke 1:41 where Scripture records, "And it happened, when Elizabeth heard the greeting of Mary, that the babe *(brephos)* leaped in her womb; and Elizabeth was filled with the Holy Spirit." The other is found in Luke 1:44, "For indeed, as soon as the voice of your greeting sounded in my ears, the babe *(brephos)* leaped in my womb, for joy." Note in each of these cases, the brephos (baby) is still in the womb. It is blatantly clear that God considers an unborn baby more than simply a wad of tissue. He considers the *brephos* as much a human being as the child who is already born and playing, running up and down the street. In God's vocabulary, the little package of love in the uterus is a *brephos* just as much as the toddler in the playpen! He uses the same word to identify them both.

There is even a sense in which the issue of life goes back beyond science and Scripture. Yes, back even before conception into the Eternal Councils of Creator God. God deals with us not only after our birth for all eternity, but *before* our birth and conception and all eternity past. To Jeremiah, God said, "Before I formed you in the womb I knew you; before you were born I sanctified you; I ordained you a prophet to the nations" (Jer. 1: 4-5). "My mother might have been my grave" (Jer. 20:17). If an abortion had been performed upon the fetus in Jeremiah's mother's womb, he still would have been Jeremiah. Although his mother may not have known his name, God did! Yes, life begins even before conception in the eternal councils of God. The great apostle Paul put it like this, "Just as He chose us in Him *before* the foundation of the world, that we should be holy and without blame before Him in love" (Eph. 1:4).

Thus, if life is present at conception, as both science and Scripture certainly reveal, then as a Christian there is no such thing as neutrality. Solomon, the wisest man who ever lived, said, "Deliver those who are drawn toward death, and hold back those stumbling to the slaughter. If you say, 'Surely we did not know this,' does not He who weighs the hearts consider it? He who keeps your soul, does He not know it? And will He not render to each man according to his deeds?" (Prov. 24:11-12).

The main reason convenience abortions on demand are the law of the land is not because of the militant minority of the women liberationists and politicians, but primarily because moral people do nothing and say little as we walk by on the other side of the street ignoring this national blight. Perhaps the thing that is most amazing is the silence of the grand old flagship churches in the hearts of cities across America. Where are all the voices from all the First Baptist churches of our land? Where are the voices from the First Presbyterian churches and the First Methodist churches? Some denominations in recent conventions have even taken pro-abortion platforms and stands. Perhaps Joel asked the question best 2,500 years ago when he cried out, "Where are all the prophets and preachers weeping between the porch and altar over the sins of the people?"

The church is virtually silent today when a child who by

state law is too young to drink alcohol, too young to vote, and too young to drive a car, is at the same time legally permitted to destroy an unborn life and never even notify her parents. What kind of a nation have we become? By and large, the church and synagogue remain silent on the sanctity of life and surrender the truth of the Torah and the good news of the Gospel to the lies of the abortionists. Moses' call comes thundering down through the centuries, "I call heaven and earth as witnesses today against you, that I have set before you life and death, blessing and cursing; therefore choose life, that both you and your descendants may live" (Deut. 30:19).

What is the bottom line for you? What do you believe? Is that a human life in the womb? You would not pass by on the other side of the street while men and women were taking two- and three-year-old children and scalding them to death in hot water and simply keep silent. As Solomon said, how we need to "rescue those being led away to death."

Dr. James Dobson has astutely observed that "all the abortion arguments descend to whether one believes an unborn baby is a live human being. If you believe the unborn is a person, then all the peripheral exclusions like rape and incest become folly." Would you kill a one-month-old baby in a crib because he was a victim of rape? Of course not! Then the same baby shouldn't be killed just because he is a few weeks behind in his development still in the womb! Yes, God has "set before us life and death, blessings and curses. Now choose life so that you and your children may live."

When I was a pastor in Florida, a few abortion rights activists rallied at the Federal Court House Building across the street from our First Baptist Church in downtown Fort Lauderdale. I walked across the street to watch their demonstration and listen to their arguments. What amazed me most was the signs they carried. They bore on them the most paradoxical and hypocritical statements imaginable. In fact, our very arguments for choosing life are found in the placards and themes which they promote. They carried such signs as: "Don't impose your morality on me," "Keep abortion legal," "Keep your laws off my body," and "Keep abortions safe." As I watched them and thought about these signs, several thoughts rushed through my mind. Let's think about their slogans for a moment.

At the abortion rally, one lady, attractive and in horn-rimmed glasses, with the obvious appearance of a lawyer or professional woman, was carrying around a sign on a wooden stick which said, "Don't impose your morality on me!" Now, think about that sign for just a moment. If indeed life begins at conception, the fact is plain — abortion is a moral issue! For centuries when medical doctors have obtained their medical degrees they have taken an oath called the Oath of Hippocrates. Many doctors have it displayed on their office wall, framed beautifully and written in flowing script letters. A portion of this Hippocratic Oath states: "I will give no deadly medicine to anyone if asked, nor suggest such council, and in like manner, I will not give to a woman a pessary (instrument) to produce abortion." In listing the things which God hates, Solomon says one of the things is, "hands that shed innocent blood" (Prov. 6:16-17). As I looked at that sign, I pictured the bloody hands of a physician who took the Hippocratic Oath promising to never knowingly administer any drug that would injure life. For some medical doctors today it is no longer the Hippocratic Oath but the Hypocritic Oath!

At the rally as I looked at the lady's sign, I also pictured the blood of the innocent victim who never had a chance to "pursue life, liberty and justice" as guaranteed by our Constitution. How long will God continue to bless a nation which is so blatantly oblivious to His Word? Joel, the ancient Jewish prophet said, "Egypt shall be a desolation, and Edom a desolate wilderness, because of violence against the people of Judah, for they have shed innocent blood in their land" (Joel 3:19). Why did they become desolate? Because they "shed innocent blood in their land." And the woman continues to carry her sign — "Don't impose your morality on me!"

Choice! That is the password for the pro-choice advocates. Their cry is loud and long — "You people who are pro-life are trying to take away my power of choice. Don't impose your morality on me!" Now think about that. We are taking her power of choice? Think about the many choices that are made which lead up to so many convenience abortions on demand. Consider the choices a particular lady has already made. Should I go to the singles bar after hours? And she makes a choice — yes! Should I flirt with that man at the bar or not? And she makes a choice — yes! Should I go out with him or not? And she makes yet another choice — yes! Should I have sex with him or not? And she makes a choice — yes! Should I have sex without any preparation or birth control? And she makes another choice — yes! And then she becomes pregnant! And then she begins to scream that we are trying to take away her freedom to choose. She chose all right, and what is now in her is a live human being, and two wrongs never make a right.

She should have the character and integrity to stop saying someone is taking away her choice. She chose. It is not a question of us imposing our morality on her, but her imposing her immorality on us...and the unborn, and often asking us to pay for a federally funded abortion at the same time.

The moral principles of the past have given way in our day to situation ethics. From the movie and music industries, and from the public media we hear the selfish cries of a thousand voices calling our children to lifestyles of sexual promiscuity and premarital sex. In our classrooms, modern sex education is perpetrated upon our children, and so often without the basis of a moral standard of restraint. And the woman continues to carry her sign, "Don't impose your morality on me." It ought to have a subtitle, "I'm too busy (with government help and approval) imposing my immorality on you and your children." The same long and legal tradition that acknowledges my right to control my own body, also acknowledges the illegality of harming another person's body.

"Don't impose your morality on me." Do pro-abortionists really mean this? Are they then saying, "I am personally opposed to sex discrimination; however, if others want to discriminate on the basis of sex, that is their right. Don't impose your morality on me. I am personally opposed to racial discrimination. However, if others want to discriminate on the basis of race, that is their right. I don't want to impose my morals on them." How hypocritical can these men and women be who carry around signs saying — "Don't impose your morality on me!"

Morality is the strength of any nation. If America falls, it will not be the result of a weakened military, but the result of a weakened morality. Of course we need military strength, but more than that we need moral strength and fiber. America's hope is in a genuine repentance. God said, "If My people who are called by My name will humble themselves, and pray and seek My face, and turn from their wicked ways, then I will hear from heaven, and will forgive their sins and heal their land" (II Chr. 7:14).

In many ways, America has become schizophrenic on the issues of life. What an irony that so often the same ones who hold their signs outside our state and federal prisons promoting life for those guilty of murder and on death row, are the same ones who hold signs at abortion rallies promoting the continual slaughter of millions of innocent unborn babies in abortion clinics. Any society which allows the continual murder of its unborn will not survive indefinitely. Yes, the sign caught my attention… "Don't impose your morality on me." Can anything be more hypocritical or paradoxical? What we are seeing in our nation is that good and godly people are at last fed up with others imposing their immorality on them!

Another lady carried a sign which said, "Keep abortion legal!" Now let's think about that sign for a moment. There are many who say, "abortion is all right because it is legal." But just because something is legal does not mean it is moral or right. It is interesting what the pro-abortion people are saying about the unborn. They say that the fetus is a non-person. They say the fetus possesses no soul. They say the fetus possesses no legal rights. The fetus, in their opinion, is simply a piece of property belonging to the mother and can be disposed of at will. And, it is all legal!

Now, that sounds very familiar, doesn't it? It should certainly sound familiar to every black American. Our American history books are replete with the smudge and shame of slavery upon our nation's character. What did slave owners insist about their black slaves? They called them non-persons. They possessed no legal rights. Some even went so far in their stupidity and blindness to say they had no souls. They were simply a piece of property belonging to the master and could be disposed of at will. And, it was all legal! Does that sound familiar?

Abortion advocates are no different from slave owners in the sense that they are fighting for their rights and are ignoring what should be the legal rights of others. Thank God that good and moral people took a stand against slavery! It brought about a civil war, but they stood for what was right. Thank God today that good and moral people are once again making a stand against abortion. Not since the days of the abolitionists and of Abraham Lincoln has the conscience of America raised its voice so loud and long over such a disgraceful national practice.

Once it was legal in this country to own slaves. But that did not make it right! Thank God we came to our senses and righted this dastardly wrong. Today, it is legal to kill babies in the womb, but that doesn't make it right any more than slave laws made slavery right. We went to war in this country to right the wrongs of slavery, and political war clouds are gathering over the abortion question. It is not going to go away! Men and women of conscience are raising their voices over this shameful disgrace.

Chuck Colson reminds us of another historical example

which offers much hope. "The Christian politician William Wilberforce stood against the deeply entrenched political and economical interest in England's slave trade. He stood as well against the courts that held that slaves were nothing more than property. Despite the overwhelming opposition, Wilberforce and a small band of like-minded Christians persisted. They prayed for three hours a day, circulated antislavery literature, mobilized churches and citizens groups, and in the end they triumphed with a glorious victory that stamped out the slave trade. But what was not so glorious was the fact that their campaign took twenty years. They were defeated time and time again in the House of Commons. They were lampooned in political cartoons, and snubbed by society's elite. But they persisted and righted the tremendous wrong."

If abortion continues to remain legal in America, what will be the next class of humanity to be legally and systematically destroyed? Will it be the mentally retarded? Perhaps the handicapped? Certainly, we are already seeing signs that the elderly are next in line. Euthanasia is the Siamese twin of abortion. If the pro-choice advocates argue against bringing "unwanted children" into the world, how long do you think it will be before they begin pushing "unwanted elderly" out of the world?

The next time you see a pro-abortion rally think about the sign that says, "Keep abortion legal." Remember, just because something is legal does not mean that it is right. Our laws must be changed! One woman who has lived through years of the trauma of an abortion wrote, "If abortion had not been legal, I would not have had to live through those dark years of depression."

At the abortion rally I attended, one particular vocal and vindictive protester wore a sandwich board type of sign which read, "Keep your laws off my body!" Now, that sign sounds right. And, it is. I agree with it! I don't want the government making laws regarding my rights or health care. There are many medical decisions that ought to be personal. Some readers of this book have had plastic surgery. That is your personal decision. Some have desired to donate organs. That is a personal decision. Some have undergone different types of cancer treatment. That is a personal decision. There is nothing wrong with the desire to be free of government intervention upon our bodies. I agree with the sign that says, "Keep your laws off my body." However, for the one who is pregnant, there is no longer one body to think about — there are two!

Those who are influenced by abortion and follow the Judeo-Christian ethic have a dilemma in the fact that in the womb is a person whether they want to believe it or not. Consider these words of the Psalmist:

"For You formed my inward parts; You covered me in my mother's womb. I will praise You, for I am fearfully and wonderfully made; marvelous are Your works, and that my soul knows very well. My frame was not hidden from You, when I was made in secret, and skillfully wrought in the lowest parts of the earth. Your eyes saw my substance, being yet unformed. And in Your book they all were written, the days fashioned for me, when as yet there were none of them" (Ps. 139:13-16).

These words teach, without question, that which is developing in the womb is not a blob of tissue, but an expression of God's greatest creation, man!

It is God himself at work through the creative processes in a woman's body when she is pregnant. What other explanation can one give for two tiny specks of protoplasm coming together and developing into all the intricacies of the nervous system, a circulatory system, a respiratory system, a digestive system, etc. Yes, "For You formed my inward parts; You covered me in my mother's womb" (Ps. 139:13).

A human being exists at conception and not at some later point when he or she begins to look like a newborn. David said, "Behold, I was brought forth in iniquity, and in sin my mother conceived me" (Ps. 51:5). Yes, God's "eyes saw my substance, being yet unformed. And in Your book they all were written, the days fashioned for me, when as yet there were none of them" (Ps. 139:16).

Most abortion advocates describe the unborn as only a blob of tissue. They call the fetus a "conception product." No wonder the lady carried the sign which said, "Keep your laws off my body." But the Creator doesn't see a blob of tissue in the womb, He sees a person. When Rebecca was pregnant with her twins, Jacob and Esau, in distress she called on God and He said, "Two nations are in your womb, two peoples shall be separated from your body; one people shall be stronger than the other, and the older shall serve the younger" (Gen. 25:23).

The abortionists tell us that removing the fetus is no different than removing a blood clot. But God did not see a blood clot in Rebecca's womb. He saw two male children. He doesn't look upon the unborn child as a body part of a mother like her spleen or appendix. In the womb God sees life, individual life. A nurse in our church tells of a turning point in her own experience. When she was working the late night shift at one of our local hospitals, a young girl was admitted with lower abdominal pain. Two days previously she had had a saline abortion. She requested to be placed on a bed pan. The nurse when removing the pan, among the clots of blood and tissue, saw a fetus of about two months. In her words, "the little heart was beating and the cord was attached as the baby was still alive. I cannot tell you how terrible I felt. I began to cry. That was not just a blob of tissue, but a human life. If only women who are pro-choice could witness an abortion, things might be so different."

Convenience abortions are on the rise today. Consider the following from nationally syndicated columnist George Will, and see what you would decide. Here is the case. "The father has syphilis, the mother tuberculosis. They have had four children. The first one was blind. The second one died. The third one was deaf and dumb. The fourth one had tuberculosis. The mother is now pregnant with her fifth child, but is willing to have an abortion. If you determine she should, she will do it. What would you decide for her? If you chose abortion, congratulations! You have just murdered Beethoven!"

Tragically, for so many unborn, the haunting words of Jeremiah 20:17 have become their epitaph, "My mother, my grave" as millions of mothers' wombs have become millions of babies' tombs. If it is right to fight for equality and civil rights for ourselves, it is hypocrisy not to do so for those who cannot speak for themselves. If it is right to regulate the way animals in our society can be killed, and to ban by law certain kinds of traps, it is sheer hypocrisy not to speak out for those who cannot speak out for themselves. If cattle cannot be slaughtered in ways deemed careless about pain, and if stray dogs and cats must be killed by law in humane ways, it is sheer hypocrisy for those who cannot speak for themselves to be totally ignored by people who call themselves humane.

Until a child is born, a baby is obviously unseen by the human eye. I am convinced that if the womb were transparent, there would be far fewer abortions. If the young pregnant girls who are having abortions could see inside and see the baby being formed, they would seldom abort. One lady wrote of an abortion she had ten years earlier at the age of eighteen. Afraid her parents would be disgraced and disown her, she sought out a doctor to perform the procedure for three hundred dollars. She said, "As I entered the clinic doors, the nurse at the desk took my name and age. She said I was eight weeks pregnant and that it was just a mass of tissue not yet formed. As I lay on the table where the procedure was about to take place, I saw a covered jar on the table close to my feet. Terror ran through me and I asked why this jar was covered up if this thing they say is inside me is just a blob of white tissue? After seeing the jar I knew deep down inside something was not told to me. I felt betrayed and sick. It wasn't until years later when I saw the fetal growth chart, that I realized why they covered the jar. The one thing I lacked was the visual knowledge of what was really happening after conception in my body. The biggest thing I had to get over was to forgive myself for what I had done. The memory will always be there." No wonder the abortionists' clinics do not want to show fetal charts as to what this "blob of tissue" looks like a few weeks after conception.

Children were visible on the steps of the courthouse at the

pro-abortion rally that day. One little girl holding her mother by one hand held a sign in the other hand which said, "Keep abortions safe." Now, think about that one. Safe for whom? Certainly not for the baby! Just how is the baby extracted from the womb? There are several methods that are used, and if one carrying the picket sign reading "Keep abortions safe" ever witnessed the trauma and tragedy of the unborn, they would never carry that sign again. Abortion is certainly not safe for the baby.

One method of abortion is commonly referred to as "D&C" (dilation and curettage). The procedure is performed by the physician inserting a spoon-shaped instrument with sharp edges into the uterus. The baby is then cut into pieces and scraped from the uterine wall. And all the while the pro-choice advocates carry the popular sign which reads, "Keep abortions safe." For whom?

Another method is the suction type of abortion. A tube is inserted in the uterus and attached to a strong suction apparatus. This creates a powerful vacuum which tears the fetus from the womb in a mass of blood and tissue. The baby is torn to pieces and sucked into a jar. And all the while the pro-choice advocates carry their sign reading, "Keep abortions safe." For whom?

The third method is used for those farther along in their pregnancy. It is commonly referred to as the saline injection. A long needle is inserted into the mother's abdomen and into the baby's sac. Most of the fluids are removed and a strong salt solution is injected therein. The helpless baby is poisoned by the solution and kicks and jerks violently. He is literally being burned alive! Generally within twenty-four hours, labor sets in and the mother gives birth to a dead baby. However, the abortionist's greatest horror comes true, when this aborted, burned baby sometimes comes forth, still alive and then must be left to die of starvation and neglect rather quietly. A registered nurse in Jacksonville, Florida, describes one such live birth. "There was a baby in this bassinet, a crying perfectly formed baby, but there was a difference in this child. She had been scalded. She was the child of saline abortion. This little girl looked as if she had been in a pot of boiling water. No doctor, no nurse, no parent to comfort the burned child. She was left alone to die in pain." And all the while the pro-choice abortion advocates carry their signs, "Keep abortion safe." For whom?

Another method is the cesarean section which is generally performed the final three months of pregnancy. Here the physician enters the womb by surgery through the wall of the mother's abdomen and then removes the baby. The baby whose lungs are often not yet adequately developed is left alone to die of neglect. And all the while the pro-choice advocate carries her sign reading, "Keep abortions safe." For whom? Recent debates in Congress include the issue of partial birth abortions for those in their final trimester of pregnancy.

Not only is it not safe for the baby, but what about the mother? Remember, we have more than one facet of our being. We are not simply talking about the physical, but also the emotional and spiritual. The truth is, abortion is never 100% safe, whether it is legal or illegal. The constant cry of the pro-choice advocate is, "Don't send us back to back alley abortions." I have watched them at their rallies carrying coat hangers wrapped in women's bras and undergarments as protest symbols. How degrading to a woman! These women must not think very much of a lady's ability to make a wise choice so as to insinuate that they are going to retreat to some back alley, take some rusty coat hanger and insert it in their body to abort their baby.

The sign reads, "Keep abortion safe." For whom? As a pastor I have dealt with the aftermath of abortion in many lives. One lady in our congregation had an abortion at the age of twenty as a result of premarital sex with her boyfriend who is now her husband. She says, "It has been over ten years and I still feel the pain and loss of it as if it were yesterday. It was a decision we reached together, one based mostly on preventing embarrassment and shame to our parents and the local church. We simply wanted to get rid of an untimely problem. The college clinic and local planning council simply set up an appointment to have a suction vacuum procedure done. Not once did anyone tell me just how my ten-week-old baby looked, or how it was growing. If only there had been someone informative with the truth from the pro-life perspective. 'If only' those words I have said a hundred times! When I had my first baby, there was both joy and sadness in my heart. Joy because of the tremendous miracle God had given, and sadness because I fully realized that there really was a baby which I destroyed earlier. It was especially difficult when I began to think how old my child would be and wondered what he or she might have looked like and been like. Time has a way of healing so many emotional scars, but abortion is a scar that is carved on my heart. And I don't think time will ever change it completely!"

Another lady wrote to say, "I became pregnant when I was sixteen. I did not want to have an abortion, but I felt I had no choice. The abortion clinic told me to lie about my age so I wouldn't have to get permission from my parents. As I was in the abortion clinic, I could hear my baby being sucked away during the procedure. I immediately felt the loss and cried. Terrible nightmares started — every night! I became obsessed with wondering what my baby would have looked like and whether it was a boy or girl. I had that abortion in 1975, and until I accepted the Lord Jesus as my Savior, my life and self worth continued to decline. But after I came to know Christ, I had a hard time forgiving myself. For me, I realized abortion does kill, not only my baby, but in a very real sense a part of me too! I honestly could say, I don't think I would be alive today if not for the Lord's forgiveness and healing." As I read that letter I thought about the lady who carried her sign that says, "Keep abortions safe." For whom?

Long ago Moses brought his people to decision with these words: "This day I called heaven and earth as witnesses against you. That I have set before you life and death, blessings and curses, now **choose life**, that both you and your descendants may live" (Deut. 30:19).

To the many who have had abortions, please read the following: abortion is not the unpardonable sin! Many live with the haunting, longing that if only that moment could be lived over again. The grief you feel is normal. You should thank God that your conscience is not seared. The good news is that Jesus Christ died on the cross to make a way for you to be free of your failure and saved from your sin. Along with our sins he also bore our sorrows and grief, our mistakes and failures. How beautiful are the words of Paul in Romans 8:1, "There is therefore now no condemnation to those who are in Christ Jesus." God is not mad or angry at you. He hates sin, but He loves you! He stands with open arms to forgive you. "If we confess our sins, he is faithful and just to forgive us our sins and to cleanse us from all unrighteousness" (I John 1:9). If you have aborted a child, God will forgive you right now if you ask him. Through His forgiveness you can know the true freedom which comes in placing Him as Lord of your life. You can purpose to follow Him, accept His cleansing, and then not call unclean what He has cleansed. You can forgive yourself! Rejoice in the fact that your child is present with the Lord and join Karen Sullivan Ables who put it like this:

> *In a far away place and a different time*
> *I killed my first child, a most heinous crime.*
>
> *The state didn't come, and I didn't stand trial.*
> *Judge Blackmun was calm when he said with a smile,*
> *"Killing is legal, say we the High Court.*
> *But don't call it murder. Just call it 'abort.'"*
>
> *The judge in my heart would not let the case rest.*
> *I had no defense when once put to the test.*
> *Found guilty I was by my heart's Supreme Court.*
> *"You murdered your baby!" they screamed in retort.*
>
> *With tears on my cheeks it was too late, I knew*
> *To bring back the life of the child I once slew.*
> *The gavel slammed down, and it rang in my head,*

"You are guilty as charged, and deserve to be dead."

"We now give you torment to pay for your sin,"
Was the sentence passed down from my own court within.
"You will never escape. You're branded. Don't hide.
Your just due is death. You should try suicide."

I was beaten in prison by daily attacks.
I was paying a debt, so I never fought back.
No hope of escaping, and this I knew well.
I cried out to God from my own self-made hell.

That day I met Jesus; He smiled in my face.
He said, "I forgive you. Come walk in my grace."
"Lord, I believe you forgive me and yet,
Blameless you are. Can you pay for my debt?"

"And, Lord, please don't touch me for I am unclean.
I'm filthy with murder; a most wretched being."
I poured out my story. He showed no surprise.
I gazed up with awe at the love in His eyes.

He said, "I paid for your crime, yes, was nailed to a tree.
There's no condemnation if you'll trust in Me.
I took on your blame and your curse on My soul
So you may be free without judgment and whole."

I sputtered, "Dear Lord, where's the justice in this?
I killed my first son, and you offer me bliss?"
Tears blurred my vision, yet there in His face
Were eyes of compassion, blue oceans of grace.

I thought to myself, "Now the past has been buried?

I'm free of the guilt that for years I have carried?"
He said to accept. It's a gift that is free.
This is atonement, not justice for me!

My judge was dismissed, my accusers, and jury.
The truth of His love made them leave in a fury.
He smiled, "Walk with Me and come learn My way,"
And grasping His hand I began a new day.

There is also a word to the physicians who have performed abortions. God's word says, "Cleanse your hands," (James 4:8). Over 2,500 years ago King David, a murderer, prayed, "Deliver me from the guilt of bloodshed, O God, the God of my salvation, and my tongue shall sing aloud of Your righteousness" (Ps. 51:14). If you repent, God will forgive you and say to you what He has said to another in Scripture, "Neither do I condemn you, go and sin no more" (John 8:11).

Finally, there is also a word to anyone contemplating an abortion. Could you murder your child on its first birthday? Of course not! That would be the farthest thing from your mind, and so should aborting the child while he or she is in the womb. There is a human being inside you. God has already named that child and he is in the process of perfecting him or her. Don't buy the argument that the child is an "unwanted child." There are many couples right now trying to adopt. Please do not do something you will regret the rest of your life. Do not destroy something that is not yours. The child in your body belongs to God, even though it may be in your womb at the present time. One lady who had had an abortion said, "I actually admire the young women in our church, who are very visible, and have had children out of wedlock. They could have taken the coward's way out to avoid the shame of a 'visible sin.' Praise God for their example to other girls that these out-of-wedlock children can be loved and accepted. I cannot look today at an 11-year-old child without the pain of realizing my child would be that age today. But when I see my baby, I realize how deeply God must love me to once again trust me with one of his little ones." Please do not take an innocent life for your own convenience sake! Regardless of what you may hear at the abortion clinic — abortion is not safe!

And to the silent majority who call abortion murder, it is time to begin acting like it! Solomon warned, "If you say, surely we did not know this, does not He who weighs the hearts consider it?" (Prov. 24:11-12). We must remember that our enemies are not people, but the Satanic system and deception behind their practices. "For we do not wrestle against flesh and blood, but against principalities, against powers, against the rulers of the darkness of this age, against spiritual hosts of wickedness in the heavenly places" (Eph. 6:12). Abortion is simply the outward manifestation of the inward problem of the heart. "For from within, out of man's heart come evil thoughts, sexual immorality, theft, murder, adultery, greed, malice, deceit, lewdness, envy, slander, arrogance and folly. All these evils come from inside and make a man unclean" (Mark 7:21-23).

Isaiah said it best 700 years before the coming of Christ when he said, "Cry aloud, spare not; lift up your voice like a trumpet; tell My people their transgression, and the house of Jacob their sins" (Is. 58:1). Isaiah was saying, get involved! Write your Congressmen. Sign petitions. Warn others that voting for abortion defiles our nation's hands with innocent blood. The real battle-field is the place of prayer. Pray for support organizations which stand for the life of the unborn. Yes, "God has set before us today life and death, blessings and curses. Now, **<u>choose life</u>** so that you and your children may live!"

Palm Sunday:
It is Palm Sunday…
is Jesus still weeping?

Luke 19:41; John 11:35

There are a lot of beautiful and awe-inspiring mountains in the world. From the Himalayas to the Alps to the Rockies, mountains have their own unique ways of pointing us to God. However, there is no more important mountain related to both past and future events in human history than is the Mount of Olives in Jerusalem. It was there on the eastern slope that our Lord made His triumphant entry into Jerusalem over palm branches a few days before His own crucifixion. It was on this mountain that Scripture records for all posterity the weeping Christ. On the eastern slope of the mountain in the village of Bethany He wept over our sorrows (John 11:35). On the western slope of the Mount of Olives overlooking the city of Jerusalem, He wept over our sins (Luke 19:41).

Many believe Palm Sunday is about the pomp and circumstance and the celebration of the hour. After all, people were shouting their hosannas and waving their palm branches. But it is not. Palm Sunday is about tears. It is about weeping. It is about crying. We have raised a couple of generations in the Western world who seem to have lost their tears. Our culture has taught us that it is inappropriate to cry. In the Broadway musical *Evita* we hear the former first lady of Argentina singing, "don't cry for me Argentina." When I was a teenager, a popular singing group called Frankie Valli and The Four Seasons had a number one hit entitled, "Big Girls Don't Cry." We tell our young sons "be a man and don't cry." One of the major problems facing our culture today is that we've lost our tears.

A brilliant ophthalmologist in one of my former pastorates shared with me the medical truth that crying is a part of an important release valve in many people. Crying may even be a chemical release for emotional stress. My physician friend said that tears actually release a chemical that helps relieve stress. This is why we often feel better after we cry. Tears have a medicinal effect. Sweat pours out of the body on a hot day to keep the body cool. Tears flow to release the stress of the soul like the sweat of the body.

As the Lord Jesus stood at Lazarus's tomb He was saying, "It is okay to cry." In fact, God gives us tears. When we think about it there are no other animal species who cry with emotional tears. Dogs don't cry. Turtles don't cry. Cats don't cry. But we do. Tears are the gift of God. Jesus is telling us on this Palm Sunday that it is okay to cry. He did Himself. This is why King David said that, "Weeping may endure for a night but joy comes in the morning" (Ps. 30:5).

On Palm Sunday I hope to etch into your memory the picture of the weeping Christ. Jesus wept! Think about that. Some are too proud to cry. Others haven't cried in years. Still others have lost their tears. But not our Lord. Jesus wept. There are two times in Scripture that record His weeping. Both of them are found on the Mount of Olives. Once, on the eastern slope when he wept over our sorrow, He is touched by our broken hearts. The other, on the western slope when he wept over our sin, He is troubled by our blinded eyes. It is Palm Sunday. Is Jesus still weeping? His tears speak volumes to us today. Let's listen to them on Palm Sunday.

It is Palm Sunday and Jesus is weeping over our sorrow...He is touched by our broken hearts

 Therefore, when Jesus saw her weeping, and the Jews who came with her weeping, He groaned in the spirit, and was troubled,

And He said, "Where have you laid him?" They said to Him, "Lord, come and see."

Jesus wept (John 11:33-35).

The event was the funeral in Bethany of his dear friend Lazarus. Note when the Lord Jesus wept. He wept when He saw Mary crying. Tears touched the heart of God. Mary's heart was broken. Her brother was dead and Jesus was too late. She held no hope. She was hurting. When our Lord arrived on the scene He saw her "weeping." John uses an interesting word in the language of the New Testament (Koine Greek) to describe Mary's weeping. The word is klaiō meaning "deep sobs, wails." Mary was pouring out her soul. Our Lord had come from a place where there was no sin, so sorrow, no tears, no tombs, no hurts, and no heartaches. Now He walks upon the scene and sees her crying with deep and loud sobs.

When our Lord saw Mary crying in such a fashion two things happened. The Bible says He "groaned" in His spirit and was "troubled." As our Lord stood at the tomb of His friend, He was indignant at what sin had done resulting in death and sorrow and in His restraint He groans and was troubled. The text tells us that what really got to Him was Mary's tears and the cause behind her heartbreak, that is, sin and death brought such great pain and to this day still brings such pain.

Now, with poignant brevity John simply writes, "Jesus wept" (John 11:35). This is the shortest verse in all the Bible and perhaps one of the deepest. Mary was upset. Our Lord knew that better than anyone. What would He do? Give her a lecture? Rebuke her? Try to encourage her? No. She wept and He wept. It's Palm Sunday and Jesus is still weeping over our sorrows because He is touched by our broken hearts. The tense of the verb tell us that He could not hold it in. This was a spontaneous expression of love. Yes, He is the "man of sorrows acquainted with our grief." The Lord Jesus is not a spectator to our heartaches. He has borne our griefs and carried our sorrows.

Some men may think that it is not good to be seen crying. However, great men are not afraid to shed tears. The Apostle Paul himself reminded those at Ephesus that he had been "serving the Lord with all humility, with many tears" (Act 20:19). And to the Corinthians he said, "For out of much affliction and anguish of heart I wrote to you, with many tears" (II Cor. 2:4). In the early days of the Salvation Army when it was a great missionary force in England, a young man assigned to a particular city wrote back to headquarters with a telegram which simply said, "Have tried everything, ready to quit." General William Booth wired him back with two words, "Try tears." Tears moved the heart of God.

It's Palm Sunday and Jesus is still weeping over our sorrows. He is touched by our broken hearts. Solomon reminds us in Ecclesiastes 3:4 that there is "a time for tears." If you need God's attention, try tears. The Psalmist said that God "keeps our tears in a bottle" (Ps.56:8). Not one of your tears falls unnoticed nor unforgotten.

Tears speak louder than words. Tears have a language all their own and need no interpreter. Any of us who have raised children know this to be true. Any of us who held our husbands or wives in a time of tears know this to be true.

Nothing moves the heart of God like tears. In the Old Testament King Hezekiah was about to die and was told to get his house in order. He prayed and wept and God replied, "I have heard your prayers, I have seen your tears" (II Kin. 20:5). Yes, tears touched the heart of God. Try tears.

Yes, it's Palm Sunday and Jesus is still weeping over our sorrows. He is touched by our broken hearts. To the government you may only be a number, a Social Security number, but you're a somebody to God. The same Lord Jesus who saw Mary's tears and wept with her stands by your side today. He is saying to us across the centuries that it is okay to cry. He is touched by our broken hearts.

It is Palm Sunday and Jesus is weeping over our sins...He is troubled by our blinded eyes

 Now as He drew near, He saw the city and wept over it (Luke 19:41).

Do you get the picture? A few days after the experience in Bethany on the eastern slope of the Mount of Olives, Jesus finds himself on the back of a donkey making a triumphant entry into the city of Jerusalem. The scene is filled with all the excitement of the cheering crowd who are waving their palm branches. Most Palm Sunday messages in most churches are about the parade, the pep rally. But all of that was a sham. And our Lord knew it. Within five days they would all be gone and their cheers would turn to jeers. Can you picture Him on this Palm Sunday morning? He is the center of attention. One would say He must have had a smile on His face. He was riding on the back of a donkey like riding in a convertible in a parade. Everyone was partying. Everyone was waving. Everyone was shouting their hosannas. But the Lord Jesus? Look at Him, "now as He drew near, He saw the city and wept over it" (Luke 19:41). Do you see Him? He is the object of their adoration. But He is weeping. Hear Him through His tears as He says, "If you had known, even you, especially in this your day, the things that make for your peace! But now they are hidden from your eyes. For days will come upon you when your enemies will build an embankment around you, surround you and close you in on every side, and level you, and your children within you, to the ground; and they will not leave in you one stone upon another, because you did not know the time of your visitation" (Luke 19:42-44).

Those Jerusalem crowds wanted a "Stormin' Norman" Schwartzkopf. They wanted a George Washington who would ride into town and put down the Roman opposition. Thus, when they did not get what they wanted, their cheers turned into jeers. Less than a week later they crowned Him a king all right but with thorns. They stripped Him naked. They beat Him until His back was a bloody pulp. And then they asked, "Are you the King of the Jews?" What a joke, they thought! And they laughed and they laughed and they laughed.

He was a king all right but His kingdom was not of this world. His was a kingdom of our hearts and so our Lord Jesus sat on the Mount of Olives and "wept." Now, these were different tears than the ones we read about in Bethany a few days earlier. In Bethany the Greek word to describe Jesus weeping was dakruō. This is the only time we find this verb used in the New Testament. It means to shed tears in such a fashion that we weep silently. It is closely akin to getting a lump in our throat and having a tear or two spill out of our eyes. This is what happened to Jesus at the grave of Lazarus. However, on Palm Sunday when we are told that He wept, the Greek word we find here is klaiō. These are the same deep sobs that we find Mary using in John 11:33. This is also the word used to describe Simon Peter when he wept bitterly after the rooster crowed and reminded him of his denials. Look at the Palm Sunday road. Look at our Lord. The people are cheering. They're waving their palm branches. But He broke down and cried with deep sobs that could be heard a block away. Yes, it is Palm Sunday and Jesus is still weeping over our sin. He is troubled by our blinded eyes. He is still saying, "How often I wanted to gather your children together, as a hen gathers her brood under her wings, but you were not willing!" (Luke 13:34).

The church in the Western world today does not seem to be weeping over the sins of the people. We do not seem to be troubled by blinded eyes. We are watching the decay of a civilization before us. A few years ago when I was a child we used to read about shoot-outs in Dodge City and today we read about them in the school buildings of our land. A few years ago when I was in school problem students were those involved in talking out of turn, chewing gum in class, running in the halls, cutting in the cafeteria line, littering on the school grounds. Today the problems are drugs and teenage pregnancies and suicides and guns as well as extortions and robberies. This is America of the 21st century and Jesus is still weeping. But we are not! If we viewed our cities as our Lord sees them we would see them through our tears. The problem with the church today is that she has lost her tears. We may still cry in emotional movies or when our dog dies but the de-Christianizing of a culture does not seem to affect us!

As we wave our own palm branches on this day does this story tell us anything about ourselves? Is there anything in our lives that might cause our Lord to weep? Is He saying to any of us, "How often I wanted to gather you, as a hen gathers her brood under her wings, but you were not willing?" Are we like some of them? Shouting and supporting and waving our palm branches as long as we get what we want? Even in the midst of our own Palm Sunday, our Lord may still be weeping over our sin. He may still be troubled by our blinded eyes.

It is Palm Sunday and our Lord is still weeping over our sorrows. He is touched by our broken hearts. Just as He wept with Mary, He's touched by our own tears. It is Palm Sunday and Jesus is still weeping over our sins. He is troubled by our blinded eyes. Just as He said to those on Palm Sunday road, He says to us today, "If you had known, even you, especially in this your day, the things that make for your peace!" (Luke 19:42). Does our Lord weep with you today or over you? There is a big difference. He weeps with us in our sorrows and over us in our sin.

The last time tears were mentioned in the Bible was in Revelation 21:4. What a scene in heaven. God "will wipe away every tear from their eyes." That is the hope of Palm Sunday! Yes, in days of dusk and darkness remember that God preserves all your tears in a bottle. Why? That He may one day at dawn wipe them all away. Perhaps David said it best when he said, "For His anger is but for a moment, His favor is for life; Weeping may endure for a night, but joy comes in the morning" (Ps. 30:5).

Easter Sunday: The empty tomb and the second chance

Mark 16:7

Mark's account of the Resurrection includes two small words that make all the difference. He begins by recounting the women who came to the tomb to anoint our Lord's body for burial. To their amazement they found the tomb empty and an angelic being at the tomb who announced the resurrection. The angel informs them that the Lord is not there, but He is risen. Then, he says, "But go, tell His disciples — and Peter — that He is going before you into Galilee; there you will see Him, as He said to you" (Mark 16:7). Do you see those two words that make all the difference? Look carefully. Mark 16:7. "And Peter." There, in a sense, we have the Gospel in two words.

Why would we find this insertion — "and Peter" — in the midst of this angelic message. One might have expected that we would have found words of antagonism. That is, "Go and tell his disciples — and Pontius Pilate or Herod or Cephas" or any of the others who played a part in His indictment and conviction. Or, perhaps one might have expected to find words of appreciation. In other words, "Go and tell the disciples and John." After all, John had been there at the cross with the mother of Jesus when all the others had forsaken and fled. In this same vein of appreciation he could have added the names of Nicodemus or Joseph of Arimathea or Andrew or any number of others. But these were not words of antagonism nor appreciation, these were words of affection. Our Lord knew Peter's heart. Peter had denied the Lord in his hour of testing and he was in dire need of a word of encouragement, a new beginning, a second chance.

Perhaps some of us on this Easter Sunday morning have blown it. What is the message of the empty tomb? It is the message of the second chance. Many of us are faced with setbacks or sorrows. Is there anyone on Easter morning who needs these two words — "and Peter"? Easter means hope, a new start, a new life, a new opportunity, a new beginning.

These two little words — "and Peter" — reveal that the second chance is possible, it is personal, it is private, and it is profitable.

The second chance is possible

How is this second chance possible? Because of the Resurrection. If there were no Resurrection of our Lord there would be no Gospel, no good news, no new beginning. Those two words — "and Peter" — came like water to a man dying of thirst. Peter thought the Lord would disown him. He had failed so miserably. Talk about good news, when Peter heard those words he knew that the second chance was possible.

The Bible is the story of men and women who received a second chance. When it came time to deliver a nation, who of us would have picked a murderer? But God did. Moses had blown it. Forty years on the backside of a desert prepared him to be the emancipator of his people. When the Lord spoke to him from a burning bush, he knew the second chance was possible. And what about the fellow that was so full of lust? Who of us would have ever said that a guy like that could have a heart after God's own heart? However, when we read King David's prayer of repentance in Psalm 51 we see that a second chance is possible. And what about Jonah? We all know his story well and remember how "the word of the Lord came to Jonah the second time" (Jon. 3:1). He too found that a second chance was possible.

Some may read Mark 16:7 and say, "Oh, I'm okay." But remember, before Simon Peter heard these words he had gone out and "wept bitterly." When the rooster crowed the coming dawn after his denial, his heart was broken as he was reminded of his sin. How long were his sleepless nights thinking of his cowardice and failure? Simon Peter denied that he even knew the Lord Jesus Christ. Now, his heart was broken. Can you imagine what he must have felt when he heard the angelic message that they were to go and tell his disciples — and Peter — that he was going before them into the Galilee?

The second chance is possible. No one said it was automatic! Judas did not get it. He reformed but he did not repent. The rich young ruler didn't get it. He was remorseful and went away "sorrowful" but there's no record that he repented. Pontius Pilate regretted his evil deed but we know nothing of his repentance. This verse is not for those who may think they can keep on in the same sin and come back time and time again. It is for men and women like Simon Peter who have repented, who have recognized their sin and wept bitterly over it.

The Lord Jesus did not have a private meeting with Simon Peter because he was a big sinner and guilty but because he was penitent and sorrowful. It was not his cursing and denial that brought him mercy, it was his tears. It was his tears of repentance. There's no hope for the second chance for one who's simply sorry he got caught but only for that one with a truly repentant and broken heart.

There are not many second chances that exist in the world. The good news is that with God there's always an opportunity for the second chance. Ask Simon Peter. Even the angels wanted Peter to know that the second chance was possible. The angels said to "be sure and tell Peter that he is not out, he gets to bat again!" They wanted Peter to know that one failure doesn't make a flop.

Easter means hope. It means a new life, a new start, a land of beginning again. Yes, the second chance is possible. "Go and tell the disciples — and Peter!"

The second chance is personal

The love of Christ singles us out by name. He loves us individually. He "calls his own sheep by name" (John 10:3). This was a personal message. I believe there's a lot involved in the fact that the angel used Simon Peter's new name. It is important that the angel did not say go and tell the disciples "and Simon." That was his old name. The first time Jesus saw him He referred to him by his old name but said you will be called Petros, Peter, a rock! Jesus saw the potential that was in this Galilean fisherman. Some might have expected the message to be "Go and tell the disciples — and Simon." After all, he had been living by his old nature. But our Lord used the new name He had given him. He said to go and tell "the rock" that He was risen. When Simon Peter heard that, he knew the Lord Jesus still believed in him. Put yourself in his place. He had failed. He had failed miserably. But our Lord still believed in him. He still had potential. What good news!

It is one thing for us to believe in Him, but to know He believes in us is quite an affirmation. When the employee knows the boss believes in him he gives his best. When the athlete knows the coach believes in him he strives to achieve more. When a son knows his father believes in him he goes the second mile. Perhaps some of you have failed and think you are as hopeless as Simon Peter. The empty tomb shows that the second chance is not only possible but it is personal.

Can we catch the tone of the angelic message? I like to think he said to the women, "Don't hang around here. Go and tell the disciples." And then, I like to think he paused, perhaps smiled, and then added, "And especially Our Lord wants Peter to know that he has gone before you into Galilee!" What is the message here? I believe it is that God still uses people to change our world. He doesn't use super saints. He uses people like you and me. People like Simon Peter who understand that the second chance is possible and personal.

Peter's fall had been so public. When we attend a school play and a child forgets his lines all of us in the audience pull for him as though the lines were on our own lips. When we go to a little league baseball game and the young boy has two strikes on him, we begin to pull for him to get the bat on the ball. I think there was a sense in which all of heaven watched Peter fall and now it is as though they were all pulling for him to get back up. "Be sure and tell Peter that one failure doesn't make a flop. He gets to bat again!"

Sin can do a lot of things. Sin can wreck hearts and homes and plans and people. But it cannot make God cease loving you. Easter means there's hope, it means there's new life and a new beginning. There are two words that make all the difference. "And Peter." Yes, the second chance is possible and it is personal.

The second chance is private

There's an amazing verse in I Corinthians chapter 15. It tells us that when our Lord arose from the grave He "was seen by Cephas, then by the twelve" (I Cor. 15:5). When our Lord came out of the tomb, one of the first things He did was to find Simon Peter. Some things are so personal and private that they're not recorded in Scripture. Peter thought he was finished. But the Lord Jesus found him privately. We do not know what took place. It must have been quite a meeting.

What took place in that private meeting we will never know. But we can all imagine. I'm sure there were bitter tears. I'm sure there were broken words coming through quivering lips accompanied by deep sobs and long breaks of silence. I'm sure there were also many assurances of Simon

Peter's love. How do we know this is what must have happened? Most of us have been there and know that the second chance is private.

What tender consideration we see in our Lord. He meets Simon Peter alone before seeing him with the twelve. Can you imagine how painful it would have been for Simon Peter to have first seen the wounds of Christ publicly? Can we imagine how impossible with all the others around to pour out our love and remorse in a public setting? Even though Peter had denied Christ publicly, he was forgiven privately.

Do we know anything of this private encounter? It is not enough to simply hear the good news of the Resurrection and know that the second chance is possible and personal. It comes when we have a private encounter with the risen Lord.

The second chance is profitable

This meeting transformed Simon Peter's life. He went on to Pentecost and after that to become the undisputed and recognized leader of the early church. We see him over and over in the book of Acts saying that "He cannot help but speak the things he's seen and heard." We see him beaten and imprisoned and counted worthy to suffer shame for Christ's name. And, all because of those two words — "and Peter."

Those two words — "and Peter" — speak volumes to us. We have a way of remembering one's failures and often forgetting their strong points. If some modern church members had been chosen to give this message they might have said, "Go and tell the disciples — but forget Peter. He failed. He tried to walk on water and couldn't. He denied our Lord three times. Yes, go and tell the disciples but forget Peter." But listen to the message, "Go and tell the disciples — and Peter — that He has gone before you into Galilee." We can get up from our failures because the second chance is profitable.

Simon Peter remained faithful to death. Before he died he wrote these words, "Yes, I think it is right, as long as I am in this tent, to stir you up by reminding you, knowing that shortly I must put off my tent, just as our Lord Jesus Christ showed me" (II Pet. 1:13-14). He was remembering an early breakfast on the shore where three times our Lord gave him opportunity to affirm his love and concluded the conversation by saying, "When you are old another will stretch out your hands and another will gird you and carry you where you do not wish. This He spoke, signifying by what death he would glorify God" (John 21:18-19). Simon Peter was restored in John 21. After those three affirmations of love our Lord said, "Follow me" (John 21:19). And Simon Peter did. All the way to his own death by crucifixion. But he was crucified upside down exclaiming he was not worthy to be crucified in the same manner as his Savior. It is not enough to know that the second chance is possible or personal or private or profitable. The real issue in the second chance is in obeying those words, "Follow me."

The Lord Jesus told the greatest story ever told about a second chance. We all know it well. It is the story of a young man for whom things had become too dull at home. The bright lights of the big city held a fascination for him so he took his inheritance and headed out. He thought he was going to find a good time but what he really found were hangovers and rip-offs and unemployment lines. Out there in the pig pen he rehearsed his speech of how he would come home and simply apply for a job as one of his father's servants, but he never got to use that speech. When he returned home his father saw him coming. He ran off the porch to meet him, and didn't point a finger or clinch a fist or cross his arms. He didn't ask where have you been? He just ran off that porch with open arms. And never were those arms wider than when they were open on the cross of Calvary for us. What precious words — "and Peter."

What does all this say to us on this Easter morning? It reminds us that God is the God of the second chance. Look at Job. He's down now but he'll be back. He's hurting now. But he'll be back and restored again. Look at Abraham. He's lying about Sarah now but he'll be back and be referred to as a friend of God. Look at Jonah, he may be running now but he'll be back and he will head to Nineveh and see one of the greatest revivals in recorded history. Look at David, he's blown it now but read Psalm 51 and understand why he was called the man after God's own heart. Look at Thomas, he may be doubting now saying, "Unless I see in His hands the print of the nails, and put my finger in the print of the nails, and put my hand into His side, I will not believe" (John 20: 25-26). But he'll be back and he'll end up in India meeting a martyr's death. Look at James and John. They may be jealous now in arguing over which of them would be greatest in the coming kingdom but they'll be back. One of them will die a martyr's death and the other will give us the Apocalypse. Look at John Mark. He may be quitting now and going home from that first missionary journey. But he'll be back, encouraged by Barnabas and received by Paul and he will leave us the Gospel of Mark. Look at Peter. He may be cursing now and denying he ever knew Christ now, but he'll be back. And he'll meet Christ for a second chance. He'll be back and become the undisputed leader of the early church. The second chance is profitable. Thank God He can use us even if we've messed up in the past. He is the God of the second chance.

Is there anyone who has failed? Listen to these words a final time, "Go and tell the disciples — and Peter — that He has risen and gone before you into Galilee." The Lord wants to put your name in this very verse. Perhaps Louisia Fletcher Tarkington said it best when she said,

> *"I wish there were some wonderful place*
> *called the land of beginning again*
> *Where all of our mistakes and heartaches*
> *and all of our selfish greed*
> *Could be dropped like a shabby old coat at*
> *the door and never put on again."*

Thank God there is such a place. This second chance is possible. It is personal. It is private. And it is profitable! Yes, two words make all the difference — "and Peter"!

Graduation Day

Genesis 39:1-23

I'm reminded on this graduation day of a scene that took place in a similar setting on a particular graduation day over 50 years ago. Shortly after World War II, the legendary Sir Winston Churchill of England was to be awarded an honorary doctor's degree from Yale. On the same day Yale was awarding an honorary degree to one of their own graduates. Both of the honorees were to address the graduating crowd. The Yale alumnus received his honorary degree first and began what was supposed to be a brief response. He spoke at length about his days at Yale and then began an address related to an acrostic of his school's name. He spoke of the fact that "Y" stood for youth. He then went on about the virtue of youth. He then began to speak about the "A". A, he said, was attitude and thus he began a diatribe about having the proper attitude in life. He moved on to "L" and spoke of the importance of loyalty. Finally, after a long period of time he got to the "E" which he said was for excellence and upon which he continued to elaborate on the importance of excellence in life.

When the gentleman had finally finished, Sir Winston Churchill was called forward and presented with his honorary degree. He began his response by exclaiming to the crowd, "I suppose we should all pause and give thanks that the previous speaker was not a graduate of the Massachusetts Institute of Technology!" Thus, taking a cue from the late, great Sir Winston, we will seek to be brief and to the point.

The cap and gown you wear on this day of graduation has tremendous significance. It finds its roots in ancient Greece when formal education was primarily for the very rich or the very determined. On a given day at a given graduation, a particular banquet hall in Athens was filled with royalty dressed in their finest. The great moment came when the students were to enter the hall with their beloved teacher. The wise teacher had dressed the graduates not in their garments of nobility, but in simple robes of sackcloth and had each one of them carrying a mortar board, the mark of a common laborer.

When challenged by parents and others the teacher replied, "Your sons are dressed in the clothing of the mason for their destiny is to build. Some will be architects and build cities. Some will be teachers and build lives. Some will be physicians and restore bodies. But all will be builders on a solid foundation of knowledge."

And thus to this day you wear a cap and gown to proudly symbolize the value of education and the fact that we're all builders of our own future and the future of those who come after us.

It is said of Joseph in the Old Testament that "the Lord was with Joseph and he was a successful man" (Gen. 39:2). Few people in world history have risen as high and as quickly as did Joseph. He began at the age of many of you and by the time he was 30 years of age, he was the virtual prime minister of Egypt, the most progressive nation of the world in its day. In Genesis 37 Joseph had received a dream. He saw a vision of what his life could become. He saw himself as a leader and he never lost sight of that dream. The Lord was with him and he became a successful man.

Success is a subject that's taken on a different twist in our modern culture. Many determine success by what they drive or where they live or how high they may climb in worldly circles. My pastoral predecessor at the First Baptist Church in Dallas, Dr. George W. Truett, defined it better than anyone I've known. He said, "Success is the ability to find the will of God for your life and to do it." This is true success in life.

Along the journey of life as you leave this place today, you will find three great enemies to success. One is discouragement. We get a dream and along the way we meet a few obstacles and become discouraged that we will ever be able to attain our goal. Another is diversion. All of us know people who've had a dream only to be diverted to a different path to see that good is often the enemy of the best. If we overcome the enemies of discouragement and diversion then we're faced with the enemy of doubt. Along the way, if we do not reach our dream by our own time schedule, we begin to doubt that we ever received the dream from God in the first place. Was it simply a youthful ambition or was it a dream implanted in our hearts from above?

Young Joseph faced all these enemies of success in Genesis 39 and speaks to us today across the centuries challenging us to follow his example that it might one day be said of us "the

Lord was with us and we became successful." Let's look not only at these enemies of success but their antidotes as well:

When tempted to discouragement – face God-allowed difficulties

 Now Joseph had been taken down to Egypt. And Potiphar, an officer of Pharaoh, captain of the guard, an Egyptian, bought him from the Ishmaelites who had taken him down there.

The Lord was with Joseph, and he was a successful man; and he was in the house of his master the Egyptian.

And his master saw that the Lord was with him and that the Lord made all he did to prosper in his hand.

So Joseph found favor in his sight, and served him. Then he made him overseer of his house, and all that he had he put under his authority.

So it was, from the time that he had made him overseer of his house and all that he had, that the Lord blessed Egyptian's house for Joseph's sake; and the blessing of the Lord was on all that he had in the house and in the field.

Thus he left all that he had in Joseph's hand, and he did not know what he had except for the bread which he ate. Now Joseph was handsome in form and appearance (Gen. 39:1-6).

Look at Joseph. Earlier he had received the dream of what he was to become. However, nothing was going right for him. His goal in life seemed a million miles away. His brothers, filled with jealousy and envy, threw him in a pit, stole his coat of many colors, slew an animal and spread blood on it, and then returned to their father exclaiming that Joseph must have been attacked by an animal and killed. Father Jacob lived those many years thinking his favorite son was dead. As though that were not enough, the brothers then sold him to the Ishmaelites who were in a caravan going down into Egypt. They took young Joseph to Egypt and put him on an auction block where he was sold as a slave. He was purchased by Potiphar, an officer of Pharaoh and captain of the guard. Nothing seemed to be going right for Joseph.

What do we do when we're faced with discouragement? Many of us want to give up. Some of us are like Job and we fear it. He said, "For the thing I greatly feared has come upon me" (Job 3:25). Others of us find ourselves acting like Elijah and we frown about it. We see him under a juniper tree in a moment of discouragement, even contemplating suicide. Some of us fume about it. We're reminded of the elder brother who was "angry" and would not go in to the party. Others of us are like Moses and we simply fuss about it. And then, there are a few of us like Jonah who simply flee, we run in the opposite direction!

When faced with discouragement Joseph gives us the antidote. Face God-allowed difficulties. Joseph became faithful over little things in the house of Potiphar. He faced his God-allowed difficulties and the Bible says, "the Lord was with him…and made all that he did to prosper" (Gen. 39:3). It even reminds us that "the Lord blessed the Egyptian's house for Joseph's sake" (Gen. 39:5). Could it be that God allows difficulties in our own lives to come our way so that He cannot only bless us but make us a blessing to others? Along the way to success in life we all meet up with the enemy of discouragement. When it comes, and it surely will, learn a lesson from Joseph on this graduation day and face your God-allowed difficulties with faithfulness.

When tempted to diversion – flee godless desires (Gen. 39:7-18)

 And it came to pass after these things that his master's wife cast longing eyes on Joseph, and she said, "Lie with me."

But he refused and said to his master's wife, "Look, my master does not know what is with me in the house, and he has committed all that he has to my hand.

There is no one greater in this house than I, nor has he kept back anything from me but you, because you are his wife. How then can I do this great wickedness, and sin against God?"

So it was, as she spoke to Joseph day by day, that he did not heed her, to lie with her or to be with her.

But it happened about this time, when Joseph went into the house to do his work, and none of the men of the house was inside,

That she caught him by his garment, saying, "Lie with me." But he left his garment in her hand, and fled and ran outside.

And so it was, when she saw that he had left his garment in her hand and fled outside,

That she called to the men of her house and spoke to them, saying, "See, he has brought in to us a Hebrew to mock us. He came in to me to lie with me, and I cried out with a loud voice.

And it happened, when he heard that I lifted my voice and cried out, that he left his garment with me, and fled and went outside."

So she kept his garment with her until his master came home.

Then she spoke to him with words like these, saying, "The Hebrew servant whom you brought to us came in to me to mock me;

So it happened, as I lifted my voice and cried out, that he left his garment with me and fled outside" *(Gen. 39:7-18).*

Most of us are familiar with this story. Potiphar's wife begins to lust after young, handsome Joseph. She begins her seductive way with him. Having overcome the enemy of discouragement he's now faced with the enemy of diversion. After all, he was a long way away from home. Nobody would surely know if he succumbed to this temptation. This type of diversion has kept many people from ever reaching their dreams.

Joseph resisted. The reason he was able to resist was became he said no from the very beginning. The Bible says, "He refused!" (Gen. 39:8). Joseph was smart enough to realize that moral earthquakes don't just happen, they're preceded by secret faults. Earthquakes don't just happen. They are preceded by fault lines way below the earth's surface, unseen to the naked eye, but which build up pressure and converge until an earthquake erupts. And so it is morally. Moral earthquakes don't just happen! They're preceded by secret faults, little cracks in character below the surface of life which begin to merge and build pressure until they too erupt into a moral earthquake. Joseph was an overcomer because he said "no" from the very beginning.

There's an interesting insight here to those who are diverted in life. Potiphar's wife passed through four stages. She saw. She coveted. She took. And she hid. These are the same four steps that anyone takes who finds their way diverted from success in life.

First, she saw. She "cast longing eyes on Joseph" (Gen. 39:7). Then, she coveted. "She spoke to Joseph day by day" (Gen. 39:10). Then, she took. "She caught him by his garment saying, 'Lie with me'" (Gen. 39:12). Finally, she hid. She sought to cover over her own sin by passing the blame and lying to Potiphar. She said, "The Hebrew servant whom you brought to us came in to me to mock me" (Gen. 39:17-18). She accused him of trying to rape her and exclaimed that she had ripped his shirt off when she fought him off.

Anyone who's ever been diverted from success in life has taken these same four steps. And it all began with Adam and Eve. She saw that the tree was good for food. Then she coveted. She saw "that it was pleasant to the eyes, and a tree desirable to make one wise" (Gen. 3:6). Then she took from the tree and ate. She also gave to her husband and he ate. Finally, she hid. When we find God coming in the cool of the day to mend their broken relationship, "…Adam and his wife hid themselves from the presence of the Lord God among the trees of the garden" (Gen. 3:8). The same is true of King David and his diversion with Bathsheba. It began when he saw her bathing on the rooftop. Then he began to covet her. He sent his servants to inquire as to who she was. Then he took her into the palace and lived in adultery with her. Finally, he also hid by trying to cover his sin, putting her husband Uriah in the front lines of battle where he lost his life.

What would Joseph do when tempted to diversion? Look at him as he flees his godless desires. "And so it was when she saw that he had left his garment in her hand and fled outside" (Gen. 39:13). He got out of there! He fled! He didn't try to fight it. He didn't try to faith it. He was single-minded. He had a dream and he would not be diverted!

As you embark on a new era of life today you will be tempted to discouragement. Face your God-allowed difficulties. And when you're tempted to diversion, flee your godless desires. Finally, we see that Joseph faced one other great enemy of success.

When tempted to doubt…follow your God-given dreams (Gen. 39:19-23)

 So it was, when his master heard the words which his wife spoke to him, saying, "Your servant did to me after this manner," that his anger was aroused.

Then Joseph's master took him and put him into the prison, a place where the king's prisoners were confined. And he was there in the prison.

But the Lord was with Joseph and showed him mercy, and He gave him favor in the sight of the keeper of the prison.

And the keeper of the prison committed to Joseph's hand all the prisoners who were in the prison; whatever they did there, it was his doing.

The keeper of the prison did not look into anything that was under Joseph's authority, because the Lord was with him; and whatever he did, the Lord made it prosper (Gen. 39:19-23).

Now we find Joseph thrown into prison for something he never did. Can you imagine what must have been going through his mind? Not too many months earlier he had received his dream, his vision. He would be the ruler of a great nation. But now? He was in prison. Could this be the reward for his faithfulness to God? Did God really give him that dream and that vision for success or was it simply some childhood ambition?

The truth is God was testing him. Psalm 105:17-19 says:

He sent a man before them — Joseph — who was sold as a slave.

They hurt his feet with fetters, he was laid in irons.

Until the time that his word came to pass, the word of the Lord tested him.

God was going to use him in a mighty way and was testing him to see if he could be entrusted with a thing as valuable as success. Often when our goals seem so far away, we too pass through a testing time and are tempted to doubt.

What would Joseph do? Surely he was tempted to doubt but he followed his God-given dreams. He did not open his mouth. He simply became faithful in the prison and before we know it, he is put in charge of the entire prison. The Lord was with Joseph!

The enemy had lost when it had tried to attack him in his body and now it tried to attack his mind. This enemy of doubt comes to so many. Abraham had been promised he would be the seed of many nations but he was old and his wife was past childbearing age and barren. How could it ever come to pass? He'd been told to look at the stars of the skies and his seed would be numbered as they. He was tempted to doubt, but he followed his God-given dream.

As you go from this place, get your dream from God. Make sure it's from Him and follow it. Abraham followed the voice of God. Joseph followed the dream of God. Joshua was the first one who got his dream the way we do. He said, "This Book of the Law shall not depart from your mouth, but you shall meditate in it day and night, that you may observe to do according to all that is written in it. For then you will make your way prosperous, and then you will have good success" (Josh. 1:8).

Have a dream. Have a dream. Have a dream. And follow it! And when you're tempted with discouragement, face your God-allowed difficulties. When you're tempted with diversion, flee godless desires. And when you're tempted with doubt, follow your God-given dreams that it might be said of you as it was said of Joseph, "that the Lord was with you and you became a successful person!" After all, success is the ability to find the will of God for your life and to do it.

Mother's Day:
Modern day motherhood

Genesis 21:14-21

Mother's Day. Those words have a special warmth to them. For many they conjure up an image of a Norman Rockwell kind of world where life is simple and everyone lives happily ever after. It frames a picture of a nice home in a neatly trimmed yard behind a white picket fence where life is filled with family fun and picnics. We like to think of a world where everyone dresses up on Sunday morning and walks to the white frame church house on the corner in a tranquil, calm and sterile environment. And, of course, we all live happily ever after. However, Mother's Day in our 21st century culture awakens to a different world than the Norman Rockwell days of a couple of generations ago.

God's plan for the home has never changed. His ideal is still one man for one woman for life. Divorce should never be an option for two believers who have been joined together as one. The Bible is plain when it comes to the teaching of the home. It doesn't teach about safe sex, it teaches about no sex until we're married. God's ideal is for the husband to be the provider and for the mother to build the nest and nurture her children. The breakdown in American moral fiber is the breakdown in the home. In our Western world we are reaping the results of a couple of generations who've been raised by modern parents who have in many cases and many ways forgotten their own roots.

Yes, the ideal family still consists of a father and mother who prays and plays with their children. But the church must not close its eyes to the reality that is all around us. We don't live in a Norman Rockwell world. All the streets in our cities are not swept spotlessly clean every night. There is not an ice cream shop on every corner, we do not see happy faces and wide smiles at every turn of the road. Many of us do not live happily ever after in a castle on a cloud. We live and minister in the real world where dreams are dashed and hopes are smashed. We live and minister in a world where people struggle simply to keep going. In our world two out of every three mothers work outside the home. Four out of five have school-aged children. The real tragedy of our day is that so many of our churches ignore the plight of many modern mothers and continue to minister like they did in generations gone by. One of the great challenges facing the church in our day is the balancing of family ministries. On the one hand we're to hold up high and holy standards of the godly home. We need to build a wall as high as we can and as thick as we can to keep people from falling over the cliffs of divorce, over the cliffs of broken homes. But, at the same time we need to keep plenty of gasoline in the ambulance at the bottom of the hill to bind up lives that are battered and hearts that are broken.

Have you looked around you lately at the world we've been called to reach? I grew up in east Fort Worth, Texas in a neat and clean frame home on the corner of a lot, with a dad and mom who loved each other, who disciplined me, and who were married for 50 years. I did not grow up watching MTV nor many of the sitcoms children watch today, which in a myriad of ways make light of the home. I grew up watching television shows like: *Make Room for Daddy*. However, in scores of thousands of homes in America today, daddy is not there to make room for. And in many of those homes it's not always his fault. He would like to be. We exist as a church for those who are not here yet. A number of those who are outside the church are single working mothers with broken hearts and broken dreams. In our modern society the real heroes are Christian mothers who are being both mom and dad. Some of them are working two jobs while at the same time going to ball games, driving car pools, cleaning houses, mowing yards and trying to keep their kids in church.

In many ways Mother's Day is a difficult time for a lot of people. There are a lot of moms in the Bible we can hold up as role models on Mother's Day. There is the virtuous woman of Proverbs 31. There's Naomi, Hannah, the Shunamite woman, Ruth, the Virgin Mary. But on this Mother's Day we bring to center stage a woman who is seldom mentioned. Her name? Hagar. My hat is off to her on this Mother's Day. Hagar teaches us a lot about overcoming, especially in the world of single motherhood. She was young and attractive. She was hardworking. She got pregnant before she was ready. Her husband abandoned her and her son. She lost her job. She had no friends and her family was a long way away. But God came to her side and to her rescue.

Hagar's story tells us how each of us can overcome. Across the centuries she speaks to us of the plight of many modern mothers, the fight of many modern mothers, and the might of many modern mothers.

The plight of many modern mothers

 So Abraham rose early in the morning, and took bread and a skin of water; and putting it on her shoulder, he gave it and the boy to Hagar, and sent her away. Then she departed and wandered in the Wilderness of Beersheba.

And the water in the skin was used up, and she placed the boy under one of the shrubs.

Then she went and sat down across from him at a distance of about a bowshot; for she said to herself, "Let me not see the death of the boy." So she sat opposite him, and lifted her voice and wept (Gen. 21: 14-16).

In Genesis 21:14 we see her hurting. Hagar was the victim. Her fate was not her fault. It was a result of Abraham's own impatience and his manipulation. It was a result of his refusal to believe God in the first place. And so he sent Hagar and their young son away. We see her hurting in these verses.

Abraham was not a bad man. He made mistakes. He got into situations and had to make some hard choices. He loved Ishmael, his son by Hagar, and there was no real joy in this separation. The Bible simply says he "sent her away" (Gen. 21:14). These were tough words. She knew how it felt to be rejected. So did the boy. He loved his dad but his dad "sent him away." Talk about hurting. Hagar was on her own. This was new to her. There was no one to help, no one to make decisions, no one to fix the car or the faucet. The Bible tells us that she "wandered" in the wilderness. She had no real direction. She did not know where she was going nor what she was going to do. Her purpose in life had been lost. This is the plight of many modern mothers. Do you see Hagar hurting? She had been sent away, rejected, and now she's on her own. Many modern mothers can identify with her today.

We not only see her hurting but we see her hungry (Gen. 21:15). The Bible says "the water in the skin was used up, and she placed the boy under one of the shrubs." It was bad enough to be hurting but now her supplies have run out and she's hungry. Her resources have run dry. The emotional strain is complicated by physical pain. Hagar finds herself like many modern mothers. She is hurting without protection and hungry without provision.

Hagar's plight is the plight of many modern mothers. Next, we see her hopeless. "She went and sat down ... and lifted her voice and wept" (Gen. 21:16). She put the boy under a tree and went off a distance from him so he could not see her. Does anyone identify with her on this Mother's Day? Is there anyone who's gone into the privacy of a bedroom and shut the door and just sat down and sobbed? God had allowed Hagar and her son to come to the point where they no longer could endure in their own strength.

Hagar's plight is the plight of many modern mothers. Many today are hurting. They too know what it is to be "sent away," and be abandoned, and to find themselves wandering without any direction. Many today know what it is to be hungry. Their resources are gone, children have needs that cannot be met. Maybe today it is not so much physical as much as it might be social or emotional hunger, and especially spiritual hunger for a companion. Other modern mothers see themselves as hopeless. Many are at the end of their rope on Mother's Day and the only thing left to do is sit down and cry.

While this is the plight of many modern mothers we should never give up. We continue on through Hagar's story to see what happens next.

The fight of many modern mothers

 And God heard the voice of the lad. Then the angel of God called to Hagar out of heaven, and said to her, "What ails you, Hagar? Fear not, for God has heard the voice of the lad where he is.

Arise, lift up the lad and hold him with your hand, for I will make him a great nation" (Gen. 21:17-18).

In these verses we see her expectation. As she sat and wept the angel of God came to her and said, "Fear not, for God has heard the voice of the lad where he is" (Gen. 21:17). Those comforting words gave her the thread by which to hang. Those words were the crack in the door. Those words were the ray of light at the end of her tunnel. Who was this angel of the Lord? This was in fact a Christophany. This was a visit of the preincarnate Christ to this goodhearted mother. Our Lord appears many times in the Old Testament. We find Him walking in the fiery furnace. We often see that He has a way of showing up when hope is almost gone in so many people's lives.

It is interesting that the Lord tells her that He's heard the prayers of Ishmael, her son. One of the things that tugs at the heart of God are the prayers of children. This is the fight of many modern mothers. What mother and what child does not want to hear these words today, "fear not, God has heard your prayers." Do you see her expectations?

Next, we see her encouragement. The Lord told her to get up and hold the boy in her hand "for I will make him a great nation" (Gen. 21:18). How many moms are fighting today to lift their kids up? There is so much around us in our culture that strips away our pride and incentive. So many children feel worthless. They have no mom or dad to lift them up. All some young people hear around the home is how they will never amount to anything or that they are worthless. Some of them have heard it so much they begin to believe it. We have raised a generation of young people and no one is lifting them up. One of the most important things a parent can do is "lift up" their children. Do you see her encouragement? She is putting her arm around her boy. This is the fight of many modern mothers.

My wife Susie and I have seen this as one of the major points in child raising. Not a day went by in raising our two daughters that in some way or another they did not hear us say, "I'm proud to be your dad" or "I'm proud to be your mom." We tried to let them know they could do anything if they would believe and trust in the Lord. We sought to lift them up. Most children are going to believe what you tell them. We see the encouragement in this ancient mother. She's building self-esteem. She's building self-worth. She is lifting up her boy. It is a fight for many of us.

Look at Hagar. Do you see her expectation? Do you see her encouragement? Next, we see her example. She lifted him up and held him by the hand (Gen. 21:18). That is, she walked with him. She showed the way. She led by example. If you look behind the most productive lives, usually you'll find a mom or a dad who "took them by the hand" and walked with them. They were there in all sorts of circumstances and situations. They led by example.

The fight is on for many modern moms. What an example Hagar is to all of us today. We see her expectations. She's calling on God and He heard her prayers. We see her encouragement. She's lifting up her boy in the midst of a difficult situation. We see her example. She takes him by the hand and walks with him. There are millions of children in America today that are waiting for this type of example. If we're ever going to reach our modern world as the church of Jesus Christ, we must see the plight of many modern mothers and the fight of many modern mothers. Finally, we need to see:

The might of many modern mothers

 Then God opened her eyes, and she saw a well of water. And she went and filled the skin with water, and gave the lad a drink.

So God was with the lad; and he grew and dwelt in the wilderness, and became an archer.

He dwelt in the Wilderness of Paran; and his mother took a wife for him from the land of Egypt (Gen. 21:19-21).

In Genesis 21:19 we see her *provision.* "God opened her eyes and she saw a well of water." God became her provider. Abraham had given her a wine skin filled with water but God gave her a well! Do you see her provision? Here was a woman who was agonizing with no apparent resources. And all the while a well was nearby. A well is a very important thing in the desert. Hagar's condition expresses the spiritual state and condition of many modern mothers on Mother's Day; hurting, hungry, and feeling hopeless. Many are wandering without knowledge that a well of eternal life is so very near.

Think about it for a moment. The well had been there all the time but Hagar just simply did not see it. It was overlooked until God pointed it out. How many times when hope seems almost gone has God shown us a well? But, it was not enough that the well was so close in proximity. God had to open her eyes. Oh that God would open the eyes of more modern mothers and show them the well of everlasting life that has been there all the time. There are a lot of moms on Mother's Day who can testify that they would have never made it without supernatural help. The fact is, God showed them a well also.

God opened Hagar's eyes and showed her a well but she had to do three things. She had to draw the water. She had to drink it herself. And she had to pass the cup to the lad. Do you see her provision? God Himself came to her rescue.

Also, we see her *promise*. I love the words in this verse. "God was with the lad and he grew…" (Gen. 21:20). She held on to God's promise that He would "make him a great nation." Our Lord is always on the side of the oppressed. God delights in coming to the rescue of those who have been cast out. This thread is woven throughout the New Testament. There was a woman at a well in Samaria who had been cast out, yet the Lord came to her rescue. There was a man in Jericho by the name of Bartimaeus who had been cast out to the side of the road but Christ came to his rescue. There was a woman in Jerusalem about to be stoned, a castout to society but the Lord Jesus came to her rescue.

There is a strange sense in which adversity has a way of building character. Hagar had help in raising her boy. It was supernatural help! God was with her! Do you see her promise? This is the might of many modern mothers. Children who are being raised by single parents should not be jealous of those who have both parents. God has a way of giving advantage to them. God is especially with them, and for them. Often, it is the child who has known struggle and sacrifice and suffering, the child who has sat under a tree somewhere and wept, the one who has known discipline and hard work, who is better prepared for life and who climbs higher than others who have known little sacrifice.

Yes, "God was with the lad and he grew…" This is the might of many modern mothers. Christ is on their side.

Finally, we see her *persistence* (Gen. 21:21). God gave her the strength to go on and she had a lasting influence upon her boy. Until it was time for him to be married she stood with him and then she released him to his wife. A single mom in touch with God can overcome every obstacle in her path. Hagar instilled love, respect and forgiveness in her boy.

There's an interesting sideline found in Genesis 25:9. The Bible records that Ishmael and Isaac buried their father together. Think about that. Ishmael went back to show respect because of his mother's persistence. This is the might of many modern mothers. Can you see their provision? God has a way of opening their eyes and showing them a well. Do you see their promise? God is with them. Do you see their persistence?

On Mother's Day let us remember that our responsibility is to build a family unit. Thank God for the home. The home is the hope of America. Let us be bold and frank in teaching our children that God's plan is one man for one woman for life. There is no such thing as safe sex. There should not be any sex outside the marriage bond. But, let's also remember that there are so many hurting around us.

Let's remember the plight of many modern mothers. People are hurting, they are hungry, they are hopeless. Let's take our hats off to the fight of many modern mothers. Let's join in their expectations, their encouragement, and their example. Finally, let's acknowledge the might of many modern mothers. They have a supernatural provision, they live by a wonderful promise, and their persistence has a lasting influence.

Many on Mother's Day are like Hagar. Perhaps you're not a single mother. Perhaps you've never known rejection. Perhaps you're not even a mother. But like her you're "wandering" through life. There's no direction. There's no purpose. There's no peace. Follow her example. Call upon God today. He will open your eyes and show you a well. You can drink from that well and never thirst again. And he will go home with you!

Father's Day

Luke 15:11-32

Father's Day...for many it's a time for new ties, long-distance calls, Hallmark cards, and family meals. I was fortunate to have had a father who blessed me with his presence. He was always there. Football season turned into basketball season, then into track season followed by baseball season and then back to fall football again and he was always there. Even now as I pen these words my mind is flooded with memories of summer vacations, playing catch in the backyard, learning the golf swing, and a myriad of other father-son endeavors. Because he was there, life went pretty smoothly for me. His presence seems to be the common thread that was woven through my childhood experiences.

It is amazing how we go through stages in life in our relationship with our dads. Someone has said that at age four we explain, "My dad can do anything." At age seven we say, "My dad knows a lot." By age 12 we're saying, "Oh well, we can't expect Dad to know everything." At age 14 we say, "My dad is hopelessly out of date and old-fashioned." By the time we reach 21 years of age we are saying, "What should I expect? He just doesn't understand." At age 25 we begin to say, "My dad knows a little bit but not too much." By age 30 we say, "I need to find out what Dad thinks." At age 40 we ask, "What would Dad have thought?" By the time we hit 50 we're saying, "My dad knew everything!" And, at 60 years of age we usually say, "I wish I could talk it over with Dad just one more time."

There are not a lot of role models around today. However, there's one tucked away in the parables of our Lord who is overlooked because he gives away center stage to his two sons. He is the father in the story of the prodigal son and the older brother. There is much we can learn from him on this Father's Day. He parented his sons with an open hand, with open arms, with an open heart. Let's look at him and learn from him on this Father's Day.

We see him with an open hand saying, "I release you!"

 Then He said: A certain man had two sons.

And the younger of them said to his father, "Father, give me the portion of goods that falls to me." So he divided to them his livelihood.

And not many days after, the younger son gathered all together, journeyed to a far country, and there wasted his possessions with prodigal living (Luke 15:11-13).

He lets him go. James Dobson might call this "tough

love." Here's a dad who is wise enough to know that what he puts in his child at a young age determines what he becomes later. This father in Luke 15 was obviously an example in the home and gave his sons some absolutes. Therefore, there was something against which to rebel.

Dads should not only be material providers, as important as that is. Nor, should they be only mental providers, as vital as that is. They should be moral providers.

The father in our story opened his hand to his boy and let him go when the time came. He could have refused. He could have held back the inheritance. There are times when a dad knows what's best but still lets his son go. He could have denied the request. He could have blackmailed his son with the inheritance. He could have done like many modern parents today and played the comparison game…"why can't you be like your big brother?" "What are you trying to do, break your mother's heart?"

Here's a dad who was prepared to stand by what he'd put in his boy from childhood. Solomon said that we are to "train up a child in the way he should go, and when he's old he will not depart from it" (Prov. 22:6). Some parents hold their kids so tight that they actually end up losing them. He let him go. He did not send a servant to spy on the boy. As much as his heart was breaking, as much as he knew wrong decisions were ahead, we see him with an open hand saying, "I release you."

Yes, he let him go but he never gave up on him. No matter how dedicated a home may be, there are seasons of disappointments which sometimes come our way. The boy left home to be free but unfortunately became a slave. The Bible tells us that "when he had spent all, there arose a severe famine in that land, and he began to be in want. Then he went and joined himself to a citizen of that country, and he sent him into his fields to feed swine. And he would gladly have filled his stomach with the pods that the swine ate, and no one gave him anything" (Luke 15:16). How many times does this happen when we get outside our umbrellas of authority which God has placed over us. A beautiful thing happens in the story. Verse 17 says that he "came to himself." All those years of training had paid off. He said to himself, "This is not for me. I've been taught better than this." Here we find the truth of Proverbs 22:6. The boy came to his senses and all those years of training produced their intended results. I can see the father now, constantly scanning the horizon. He never gives up. He is a model father for us on this Father's Day because we see him first with an open hand. He was wise enough to know the way to keep his son was to let him go and the way to lose him was to hold him tight.

We see him with open arms saying, "I receive you!" Luke 15:20-24

 And he arose and came to his father. But when he was still a great way off, his father saw him and had compassion, and ran and fell on his neck and kissed him.

And the son said to him, "Father, I have sinned against heaven and in your sight, and am no longer worthy to be called your son."

But the father said to his servants, "Bring out the best robe and put it on him, and put a ring on his hand and sandals on his feet.

And bring the fatted calf here and kill it, and let us eat and be merry;

For this my son was dead and is alive again; he was lost and is found. And they began to be merry."

We all know the story well. The boy comes to himself and heads home. "But when he was still a great way off, his father saw him and had compassion, and ran and fell on his neck and kissed him." He ran to meet him with open arms. The boy came walking but the father came running! His love had been tough enough to release him and now it was tender enough to receive him. The boy begins his speech but he never gets to give it. The father is full of forgiveness. We see him with open arms. There were no crossed arms here. No pointed fingers nor clinched fists. There was no cross examination of where he'd been nor were there any "I told you so's." There were simply open arms.

The Bible says the father had "compassion" (Luke 15:20). This word means "to suffer with." Here was a dad who knew what the boy was going through. The boy came home with hopes of only being a hired servant but was received as an honored son.

One of the beautiful things of the story is that not only did the father receive him and forgive him but he did not hold a grudge. He could have said, "Welcome home, I'll forgive you but you've got a lot of proving to do." Now, this does not mean that restoration should be without parameters. We're not talking about a boy here who came back with the same rebellious spirit with which he left nor are we talking about a boy who simply was sorry he got caught. His boy returned home different.

Here was a son who had shown true repentance. First, this boy regretted his deed. "He came to himself and said, 'How many of my father's hired servants have bread enough and to spare, and I perish with hunger" (Luke 15:17). Next, he took responsibility and blamed himself for his actions. He was prepared to say, "Father, I have sinned against heaven and before you" (Luke 15:18). Next, he acknowledged his father's right to be displeased with him. He says, "I'm no longer worthy to be called your son." Then, he resolved to sin no more. The scripture goes on to say that "He arose and came to his father." In verse 17 he changed his mind. The result was in verses 18 and 19 he changed his heart. And in verse 20 his actions were changed. This is the way to repentance. It begins with a change of attitude which always results in a change of affection which then results in a change of action. "He arose and came to his father."

What a beautiful picture we have of this loving father. We see him with open arms receiving his son. Some relationships are strained because some will not accept the offending person's repentance. However, the Bible says that "love does not take into account a wrong suffered." Here we see a beautiful picture of our heavenly Father. How thankful we are that God does not deal with us according to our sin but according to His tender mercy when we come home to Him in genuine repentance.

Look at this model father. We see him with an open hand saying, "I release you." We see him with open arms saying, "I receive you." Finally:

We see him with an open heart saying, "I respect you!" (Luke 15:25-32)

 Now his older son was in the field. And as he came and drew near to the house, he heard music and dancing.

So he called one of the servants and asked what these things meant.

And he said to him, "Your brother has come, and because he has received him safe and sound, your father has killed the fatted calf."

But he was angry and would not go in. Therefore his father came out and pleaded with him.

So he answered and said to his father, "Lo, these many years I have been serving you; I never transgressed your commandment at any time; and yet you never gave me a young goat, that I might make merry with my friends.

But as soon as this son of yours came, who has devoured your livelihood with harlots, you killed the fatted calf for him."

And he said to him, "Son, you are always with me, and all that I have is yours.

It was right that we should make merry and be glad, for your brother was dead and is alive again, and was lost and is found."

The most notable characteristic of this dad was his presence, his transparency. He was there for his boys. No matter what either of their problems seemed to be, they had one thing in common, their father's presence. The most valuable gift he gave his sons was his presence. He showed his sons respect and opened his heart to them.

Here was a dad who reminds us on this Father's Day of the importance of keeping things in perspective. Once the party began with its celebration of the return of the prodigal boy we find his older brother was angry and would not go into the party. When his father came out to meet him with an open heart the older son complained that he had been faithful all those years and had never been given "a young goat" that he might be merry with his own friends. It is interesting that they were killing the fatted calf for the party. To sulk about a goat at a time like that was sheer folly. The older brother had lost all sense of proportion. How fortunate he was to have had a father who was focused and who came to him with an open heart.

Can you picture the scene? The party is going on and the festivities are at a high point. But where is dad? He is outside with an open heart assuring the wounded older son of three important things. His abiding presence. He said, "Son, you're always with me" (Luke 15:31). He was assuring him of his abundance provision, "all that I have is yours" (Luke 15:31). And with an open heart he also was assuring him of his own achieved purpose. "Your brother was dead and is alive again, was lost and is found" (Luke 15:32).

We do not know how the story ends. Did the older boy go into the party? Did he remain outside? We simply do not know. Perhaps the Lord Jesus left the issue shrouded in silence so that you could complete the story today.

I want to be a father like the dad we find in Luke 15. Here was a man with an open hand. He was wise enough to know that the way to keep his kids when they mature is to let them go. Here was a man with open arms. He was always ready to make a way for new beginnings. Here was a father with an open heart. He was transparent and encouraging and blessed his sons with his presence.

Everything this father tells us about fatherhood comes to a very interesting point. There may be someone reading these words who has not known a dad with an open hand or open arms or an open heart. The good news is our Lord said, "I will be a father to you, and you shall be My sons and daughters" (II Cor. 6:18). The real message on this Father's Day is about our heavenly Father. He is a loving father with an open hand. He lets us go. We're not puppets, we're people. Thus, He lets us go because the love we can voluntarily return to Him is indescribably valuable to Him. He may let us go but He never gives up! He is a loving father with open arms and never were those arms open wider than when they were on the cross. He is a loving father with an open heart. He opened it for all of us at Calvary when He who knew no sin became sin for us that we might become the righteousness of God in Him!

Yes, perhaps our Lord left the end of the story as He did without our ever knowing whether the elder brother went into the party in order that we might complete the story today. When we do we will find a loving heavenly father not only with an open hand and open heart, but with open arms to receive us.

Independence Day: America, an ecotonic moment in time

Jeremiah 8:5-22

We are the "prefix generation." We describe many things in our contemporary culture with the use of the prefix. For example, the prefix, "mega." We have megabytes, mega churches, even mega-ditto's. A prominent prefix today is "eco" as in ecotones and ecosystems. America is presently in the midst of an ecotonic moment in time. An "ecotone" is a technological word from the world of biology that describes a particular place where two ecosystems merge and blend together. I first heard of the word while living in the city of Fort Lauderdale, Florida. There is a particular place where the intercoastal waterway and the New River come together and form an ecotone. The salt water from the Atlantic Ocean flows into Port Everglades and into the intercoastal waterway. From the Everglades, just west of Fort Lauderdale, the fresh water flows through the New River making its way toward the ocean. At the particular place where this salt water and fresh water blend and merge together, an ecotone develops. Ecotones are places of tremendous possibility. Often fish lay their eggs there. Ecotones can also be very problematic to those who are engaged in the battles of ecology.

At this point in time we are experiencing an ecotonic stage in American life. Two worlds are blending and merging together at the same time. One is a modern world and the other a post-modern world. The world in which many of us in the baby boomer generation were educated is history. All the cumulative knowledge of world history will double within the next few years. Our world is transforming at breakneck speed into a post-modern era. This presents a time of tremendous possibility for those of us who can translate the message of our Christian heritage to a world that is in desperate need without changing the heart of its message. It is also a time of tremendous problems for those who are seeking to translate the gospel to our world in the same way we did ten, twenty, or thirty years ago. The western world is not so much in debate over whether the Bible is true as it is in whether it is relevant. That is, does this Book written in an ancient middle Eastern culture have any relevancy in a world where we are transplanting organs, going to the moon, and experimenting with genetic engineering. They will never know unless we deal with some of the major questions of our day.

We are living and ministering in a day when the church's influence is waning in a secular society. We are seeing the product of an entire generation that has been reared with virtually no moral absolutes in the home, in many of their schools, and tragically in many of their churches. This past Sunday Great Britain saw less than five percent of its population in any kind of house of worship. History records that civilizations which see the collapse of the home and accompanying moral values do not last past one or two generations unless a spiritual awakening occurs. In America we are watching the disintegration of a culture in our own lifetime. We have lost the concept of personal responsibility for our own transgressions, and all of our maladies have become someone else's fault.

Recently I walked through the Viet Nam Memorial in our nation's capitol. I saw name after name etched in the granite wall of young people who left their homes and never came back. Some of those names were more than just letters etched in granite; they were personal friends from my high school days. As I looked at that wall, I realized that they would be in their middle age today. If by some miracle they could step out of that wall and go back to their hometowns, they would see a world that is totally different from the one they knew. They would wonder why we have become a nation where over half of our marriages end in divorce. As they walked the streets of their small towns and cities, they would wonder why the Judeo-Christian ethic was but a memory. As they revisited their schoolhouses, they would be shocked to learn that it is now illegal for children to pray in the same classrooms where they were educated. They would be floored to realize that the Gideons could no longer hand them a New Testament on the campuses of their schools, but organizations like Planned Parenthood are often free to dispense condoms at no charge. They would be surprised to discover that in many of their small towns the traditional manger scene was no longer on the courthouse lawn. They would be shocked to see that homosexual lifestyles were legitimized and promoted by much of the rhetoric, appointments, and actions of those who live in high places. As they visited their schools, they would be shocked to pass through metal detectors and see that teenage pregnancy was rampant. Those who lost their lives at such a young age would be appalled to hear that we legally kill 1.5 million babies a year in America today through abortion. As they strolled past the vacant lots and playgrounds of their neighborhoods, they would be shocked at the way they are terrorized by gangs and drive-by shootings. As they looked around, they would wonder what happened to the male leadership which has disappeared from so many of the homes of America.

We should make no mistake about it. The United States is morally bankrupt in large part because we have been led by a liberal philosophy that has made false assumptions about two particular things; the nature of the universe, and the nature of mankind. Liberal philosophy seldom asks "why." It only asks "what." One can take almost any issue. Take the issue of drugs. Few in the liberal establishment are asking "why." Most of them only ask "what." What can we do about this problem? So we dispense free needles to try to clean up the process. This particular point is seen daily with the issue of the HIV virus and the accompanying AIDS epidemic. Not enough people in Washington are asking "why." It does not seem to be politically correct. So we only ask "what." What can we do about the AIDS epidemic? And the answers we are given are more education, how to have safe sex, and the like. We are asking "what" when we ought to be asking "why" about these major moral issues of life. Have you ever thought about why we are called "conservatives?" We are trying to conserve something. We are trying to conserve some traditional moral values that have made America what it has been in the past. These values were conserved by people asking "why" and not "what."

The prophet of old, Jeremiah, lived and ministered in a day much like ours. The nation of Judah had been blessed. They had prospered, but they forgot their roots. They forgot their God. They began to think they were indestructible, and the final result came in 586 B.C. when they were defeated by Nebuchadnezzar and taken away into Babylonian captivity. Jeremiah was a man who lived with a burden for the way in which his country had turned its back on God. He had seen the blessing. Now he observed the collapse and corruption from within. With a weeping heart he asks, "Where is the Lord, Who brought us up out of the land of Egypt?" (Jer. 2:6). Then he came straight to the bottom line by quoting the Lord Himself, "They have turned their back to Me, and not their face" (Jer. 2:27). As I read these words in this Book of all books, I cannot help but see our own America. I believe God is asking today, "Where is the Lord, Who brought you out of Egypt?"...I believe He is asking us, "Why have you turned your back to me and not your face?" Jeremiah asks four hard questions in Chapter 8 of the book that bears his name. Interestingly enough, unlike the liberalism of our day, he did not ask "what." Jeremiah asked "why." These are the four "why's" America needs to be asking herself today. There is a question for the American public, "Why has this people slidden back?" (Jer. 8:5). There is a question for the American pew, "Why do we sit still?" (Jer. 8:14). There is a question for the American politician, "Why have we provoked God to anger?" (Jer. 8:19). There is a question for the American pulpit, "Why is there no recovery?" (Jer. 8:22). Is there a recovery for the Western world?

What would happen if the people, the President, and the pastors of the United States would stand up before the American people and stop asking "what" and begin to seriously probe and ask "why." If the public would seriously ask, "Why have we slidden back?" If the people in the pew would seriously ask, "Why do we sit still?" If the politicians would seriously ask, "Why have we provoked a holy God to anger?" If the pulpits of the land would seriously ask, "Why does there seem to be no recovery?" Let's ask ourselves these questions of Jeremiah's day today:

A question for the American public: Why has this people slidden back?

 Why has this people slidden back, Jerusalem, in a perpetual backsliding? They hold fast to deceit, they refuse to return (Jer. 8:5).

Jeremiah says that the people of his nation have "held fast to deceit and refused to return." That is, they and we continue to believe a lie. America seems to be without a knowledge of spiritual things today. We hold fast to deceit and refuse to return. On February 4, 1995, *The Dallas Morning News* carried a guest column by then Mayor Steve Bartlett. He said, "Up until 30 years ago, strong moral values were a part of our daily lives and experiences. They were a part of everything that we did. But in the course of those 30 years we've walked away from those values and put them in a closet. I don't know WHY (emphasis mine) that happened. I only know that it happened." Thirty years ago? Mr. Mayor, you are right. Let us remember what happened 30 years ago. For one thing the Supreme Court struck down school prayer by prohibiting this simple invocation, "Almighty God we acknowledge our dependency upon you and beg your blessings on us, our parents, our teachers, and our country." That was it! No mention of the Lord Jesus Christ. It was just a simple petition asking God to bless four things — the students, the parents, the teachers, and the country. It is shocking to examine what has happened to those four entities over the last 30 years. The invocation struck down by the Supreme Court called for God's blessings upon "us" (that is, the students). What has happened to the American student in the past 30 years? We have the highest rate of teen motherhood in the western world. Each year one million teenage girls become pregnant. In my own city of Dallas some schools are equipped with as many as 15 nursery beds to take care of the babies that are born from teen mothers who are still in school. Should we be surprised when we have asked "what" instead of "why" throughout these years? We ask "what" can we do about the dilemmas, and so we decided to hand out condoms and forbid groups like Gideons to pass out New Testaments. The petition asked the blessing of God upon our "parents." What has happened to parenthood in America in the last 30 years? We lead the world in divorce. One and one-half million children run away from home every year. Sex abuse seems to be rampant, and the home is disintegrating. But the liberal establishment is only asking "what." The third part of the petition was the invocation of a blessing upon our "teachers." What has happened to the American education system in the last 30 years? In Stone vs. Gramm in 1980 the court decided, "If posted copies of the Ten Commandments are to have any effect at all, it would be to induce children to meditate upon them and perhaps obey, and this is not permissible. The First Amendment protects it." God forbid that a child obey one of the Ten Commandments. And the result for teachers? School violence, metal detectors, and plummeting SAT scores. The final request was a blessing of God upon our "country." What has happened to the United States of America in the last 30 years? Violent crime is up 500 times over what it was in those days. It is no longer safe to walk on many of the streets of the cities and towns of America. And, here we are asking "what." The real question is "why?" Why has this occurred? Because so many good people have done nothing.

Jeremiah goes on to say that, "My people do not know the judgment of the Lord" (Jer. 8:7). It seems as though he's speaking of America and not Judah. The judgment of God is seldom heard in any of the pulpits of America any longer. Speak of the judgment of God in the city of Washington, D.C., and you'll be scoffed and laughed out of town by the social elite. But God has not abdicated His throne. He is still in control. As Daniel says, "He still rules over the affairs of men." Ask Israel if this is true. Ask Judah if this is true. Ask Rome or the former Union of Soviet Socialist Republics. Jeremiah says that "even migratory birds know when it is time to return home" (Jer. 8:7). But Judah did not nor does America. We have less wisdom than a bird.

Jeremiah continues as though he were speaking to the issues of our own day. Hear him ask, "How can you say, 'We are wise and the law of the Lord is with us?' ...they have rejected the word of the Lord; so what wisdom do they have?" (Jer. 8:8-9). Is anything more applicable to the United States of America than these words? We have rejected the Word of God for the wisdom of man's own agenda, and we wonder why as the question comes in Verse 5, "Why has this people slidden back?" He goes on quoting the Lord Himself, "I will give your wives to others" (Jer. 8:10). Does this sound like America where over half of the marriages end in divorce? Is the judgment of God upon this nation? Jeremiah speaks of those who say, "'Peace, peace!' When there is no peace" (Jer. 8:11). Those in Washington put their spin doctors on every issue saying, "'Peace, peace!' When there is no peace."

Jeremiah speaks to his people and so poignantly to us about the greatest tragedy of all when he says, "Were they ashamed when they had committed abomination? No! They were not at all ashamed, nor did they know how to blush" (Jer. 8:12). This is our greatest tragedy. There seems to be no shame. There is a blatant disregard in much of America for anything that is moral or pure. But we should not blame the politicians for the moral collapse of America. We need to put it where it belongs, at the feet of the church. Biblical moral standards are forgotten in an attempt to appease an immoral culture, and in some ways to "market" the church to a secular world.

It would do us all well to remember that the context of Jeremiah 8 is found in II Chronicles 34. In that particular chapter good King Josiah had begun to ask some "why's" instead of "what's." His trusted friend, Hilkiah, had discovered the Word of God which had been lost in the house of God. He brought it to the king, and a tremendous turning to God ensued. This is our greatest need, that the church would find this Book and take it to the king. The king led that nation to take a stand on the Word of God, and the country began to prosper once again.

Why is this people slidden back? That's a good question. Jeremiah goes on to quote the Lord Himself. "The things I have given them shall pass away from them" (Jer. 8:13). If God said this of Judah, the apple of His eye, why do you think He wouldn't say the same of any other nation? If America does not start dealing with the "why's" instead of the "what's," judgment is coming. America no longer believes that God controls the created order. We may give Him the occasional tip of a hat at a prayer breakfast or the like, but He by and large has no place in the affairs of men, particularly, in the places of power. The question is not "what." The question is "why." Jeremiah continues with another "why."

A question for the American pew: Why do we sit still?

 Why do we sit still? Assemble yourselves, and let us enter the fortified cities, and let us be silent there. For the Lord our God has put us to silence and given us water of gall to drink, because we have sinned against the Lord (Jer. 8:14).

Many Americans have bought into the liberal lies, media

manipulation, and public propaganda. The tragedy is the church sits by with a false confidence based on lying words saying, "Peace, peace, when there is no peace." We need to ask ourselves the question, "Why do we sit still?" It has not always been the case.

Recently while in the nation's capitol, my wife, Susie, and I walked from our hotel to the Capitol building. After passing through the rotunda, we headed down the corridor toward the House chamber. We entered a rather large room lined with statues of great Americans around the wall, and soon we discovered it was the original House chamber. In that particular room the House of Representatives met for scores of years before the larger chamber was built adjacent to it. While observing some of the statues in that great hall, we noticed a group over to the side with a guide in a red sport jacket lecturing. We moved over near the group to listen. This Capitol guide was in conversation regarding the issue of separation of church and state. He was explaining how that for the first 75 years the House of Representatives met in this room, and they opened it on Sunday mornings to an evangelical, gospel-preaching Protestant church which held services there for 75 years. He went on to explain how the First Presbyterian Church (now the National Presbyterian Church) held its Sunday services during those years in the chamber of the Supreme Court Building across the street. As I listened to those incredible truths that have somehow been buried in our nation's history, I asked myself the question — "Why do we sit still?"

Don't listen to those who say that religious principles played little part in the founding of the United States of America.

Don't listen to those who say that we were basically not built on a Judeo-Christian philosophy but on more of a pluralistic, deistic philosophy. Forever etched in the charters of the original 13 colonies is the gospel truth. Rhode Island was established in 1683, and in their charter they said, "We submit ourselves, our lives, our estates unto the Lord Jesus Christ, the King of Kings, and the Lord of Lords, and to all those perfect and most absolute laws given in His Holy Word." Maryland's charter says it was "formed by a pious zeal to extend the Christian gospel." Delaware was "formed for the further propagation of the holy gospel." When the founders of Connecticut wrote their charter, they said that Connecticut was there to "preserve the purity of the gospel of the Lord Jesus Christ." It certainly doesn't sound like Connecticut was too pluralistic in its beginnings. There's talk of Washington, D.C., becoming the fifty-first state. Can you imagine how their charter might read?

We wonder why in the words of Jeremiah we as a people are "slidden back" and we in the pew "sit still." The answer is in the fact that the salt has lost its savor. Some time ago I received a form letter from the head of Americans United for the Separation of Church and State in which he was bemoaning the fact that some Christian ministers in America were trying to, in his words, "Christianize America." I am unapologetically trying to Christianize America and the entire world for that matter! This is the commission our Lord gave us before He left. One of my pastoral predecessors at the First Baptist Church in Dallas, the late and great Dr. George W. Truett, stood on the Capitol steps of our nation on May 16, 1920, and gave one of the greatest messages on religious liberty ever heard. In the course of his message, he said, "The one transcending and inspiring influence in victory is the Christian faith. Civilization without Christianity is doomed. Let there be no hesitation nor apology for the insistence that the one hope for the individual, the one hope for society, for civilization, is the Christian religion." That doesn't sound like tolerance to me.

Jeremiah's question comes thundering down through the corridors of the centuries to us today — "Why do we sit still?" America's biggest problem is an apathetic church who has lost her first love. And in losing that first love, we have also lost our influence. We have simply sat still for a generation. When I see certain political leaders with their own agendas contrary to the Word of God coming out of church on Sunday being photographed with Bibles in their hands and waving to the television cameras, the words of Jeremiah 7:9-10 echo in my mind — "Will you steal, murder, commit adultery, swear falsely, burn incense to Baal, and walk after other gods whom you do not know, and then come and stand before Me in this house which is called by My name, and say, 'We are delivered to do all these abominations'?" In the midst of a changing ecotonic world that can go either way, we must stop asking "what" and begin to ask "why." Why are we slidden back? Why do we sit still? Jeremiah continues with another question.

A question for the American politician: Why have they provoked me to anger?

 Listen! The voice, the cry of the daughter of my people from a far country: "Is not the Lord in Zion?

Is not her King in her?" "Why have they provoked Me to anger with their carved images — with foreign idols?" (Jer. 8:19).

God asks us another question through Jeremiah's prayer— "Why have they provoked me to anger with their carved images, with foreign idols?" America did not abandon God. We just made Him one of many others. New Age humanistic thought which exalts man over Christ has taken center stage. It is no wonder those with liberal agendas do not want the Ten Commandments in the classroom. The very first one says, "You shall have no other gods before me." He is a jealous God. We have supported a pluralism which tolerates a form of Christianity that does not make any demands on a culture. It is a form of Christianity that only asks "what" and never asks "why." Christianity is not just another person's opinion. It is objective truth. We have provoked a holy God to anger in that we have allowed other gods to share His glory.

How did the early Christians engage their culture? What was it about them that caused the Roman Empire to put them to death in the Coliseum and other places of public exploitation and execution? Why the Christians when other conquered peoples of the world did not meet the same fate? The answer is found in one of the ruins of Rome. It is called the Pantheon, the temple of all gods. Some time ago while returning from a trip to Africa, I visited this impressive edifice. As you walk into the temple, you find around all of the walls niches carved in the stone. When the Romans would conquer a certain people who, for example, might worship the god Jupiter, they would bring them to the Pantheon and say here is a niche for Jupiter. You can worship him any time you desire. They appeased their conquered peoples in such a fashion. Perhaps they conquered a people who worshiped the goddess Juno. They would bring them there to the Pantheon and give them a niche for Juno. When they brought the Christians back to Rome in triumph of their military conquest, they took them also to the Pantheon. In effect, they said we are going to give you a niche for Jesus here between Jupiter and Juno. The Christians said no! There is only one Lord, and they gave their lives for that.

Agnostic, apathetic America has no sense that we have provoked a holy God to anger. In fact, we scoff at the idea. He says, "Do not commit murder." And we kill 1.5 million babies a year. He says, "Do not commit adultery." And we live in a sex-crazed society. When Paul wrote the Roman letter, he foresaw Rome's coming collapse, and in Chapter 1 spoke of a culture that had been given over to depraved minds.

Is there a recovery? Yes, the most important thing we can do is call upon the name of the Lord in prayer, and then begin to ask some "why's" and elect some leaders with character and genuine moral backbone. It was not the Babylonians who brought Judah low. God only used them. It was God Himself who did it. Why? The answer is in II Chronicles 28:19, "For the Lord brought Judah low because of Ahaz king of Israel, for he had encouraged moral decline in Judah and had been continually unfaithful to the Lord."

What did God do? God Himself brought the nation of Judah low. We can blame it on economics, budget deficits, the welfare system, the collapse of moral values, but God still rules in the affairs of men. There is someone in Washington not being factored into the equation. Our leadership is blind to the fact that "the Most High rules in the Kingdom of men" (Dan. 4:32). Could it be that behind all the politics is God Himself allowing all of this to happen in America?

What did God do to the nation of Judah? He brought them low. Why? Because their leader, their king, had encouraged a moral decline in the land. Ahaz was personally immoral and unfaithful, and his policies reflected his own character. It is one thing to be immoral, but another to "encourage a moral decline in the land." We have had presidents of the United States in the past who have been known for immoral acts. But it is quite another thing to encourage immorality through people and policies. A leader encourages a moral decline in the land when he takes a pen in hand and signs an executive order permitting the bodies of aborted babies to be used in research. A leader encourages a moral decline in the land when he only asks "what" and seldom ever asks "why."

Leaders of nations bear moral responsibilities, and we do ourselves a tremendous injustice if we do not elect godly men and women to leadership.

America is agnostic toward spiritual things. We seem to have an "in your face attitude" toward a holy God. There appears to be no real sense in the executive, legislative, or judicial branches of government that we are provoking a holy God to anger. So we continue on our way asking "what" when we ought to be asking "why." Why have we slidden back? Why do we sit still? Why have we provoked God to anger? Jeremiah asks the final "why."

A question for the American pulpit: Why is there no recovery?

 Is there no balm in Gilead, is there no physician there? Why then is there no recovery for the health of the daughter of my people? (Jer. 8:22).

Is there any answer? Is it too late? People in Jeremiah's day did not repent, and there was no recovery. They were taken into Babylonian captivity and hung their harps on the willow trees of Babylon because they could not sing the Lord's song in a foreign land. Jeremiah asks, "Is there no balm in Gilead, is there no physician there? Why then is there no recovery for the health of the daughter of my people?" (Jer. 8:22). Yes, there is indeed a health care crisis in America today, but it is not primarily physical nor mental. It is a spiritual health care crisis.

Is it too late for us as it was for Judah? Where is the answer? Is there no balm in Gilead? Is there no physician here? Yes, there is a Great Physician. If you go to your personal physician with a physical need, he examines you and gives you a prescription. God gives us a prescription in Jeremiah 3:22, "Return, you backsliding children, and I will heal your backslidings." Yes, thank God, there is still a Physician. The return begins with you and me. Not the politicians. Not the school systems. But with the church of Jesus Christ.

We are living in what has become more and more of a pagan culture not unlike the one with which the early church was confronted. In fact, they were under a tremendous amount of persecution we have really not seen in America as of yet. For example, in Acts 12 the leader of the church in Jerusalem,

Simon Peter, was incarcerated by the authorities for his moral stands and for the gospel's sake. Acts 12:5 says, "Peter was therefore kept in prison, but constant prayer was offered to God for him by the church." The Church of Jesus Christ has forgotten our primary battlefield. It is very difficult to win a war if we do not know where the battle is being fought. Some of us have forgotten this. That is, while Peter was kept in prison, the church was praying earnestly for him. If Acts 12:5 had been written about the 21st century church, it might read, "Peter was kept in prison, but the church picketed City Hall in behalf of him." It might read, "Peter was kept in prison, but the church protested with a mass campaign in his behalf." It might read, "Peter was kept in prison, but the church took over the local precincts in order to make some changes in the elected officials." It might say, "Peter was kept in prison, but the church signed petitions in his behalf." This early church engaged their culture. How? They had the power of God upon them. They knew where the battle was being fought. Go to Ephesus today and walk through the ancient ruins of that first century metropolis. It amazed me as I did so. As I walked through the amphitheater, down the streets, into the bathhouses and the libraries and the temples of that ancient world, I wondered, how was that city captured for Christ? Paul went there with just a couple of friends and engaged the culture and saw the transformation of a whole city. How? There was no explanation for it but the power of God. The power of God in response to a praying church. If some of us who are called by the name of the Lord would spend as much time listening to God as we do certain talk show hosts on the radio or television, we would be on our way to revival. Some of us do not think we need God because we have a conservative political agenda to follow.

There is a remedy for us. It is the only remedy, and it is not found in the ballot box or on television ads or in curriculum. The remedy is found at the foot of a Roman cross outside the city walls of Jerusalem where the conquering Christ was "made sin for us that we might become the righteousness of God in Him." We are living in the most important days of American history. It is indeed an ecotonic moment in our nation's history. Two worlds are blending and merging together. It is a time of tremendous possibility. It is not too late if — we stop asking "what?" and begin to ask "why?" There is a question for the American public. "Why are we slidden back?" We have forgotten our roots. There is a question for the American pew. "Why do we sit still?" Has an apathetic church forgotten where the battle is being fought? There is a question for the American politician. "Why have we provoked a holy God to anger?" Have we have shared His glory with other gods around us? And, there is a question for the American pulpit. "Why is there no remedy? Is there no balm in Gilead? Is there no physician there?" Yes, the Great Physician is still ready and willing to bless our nation as He did in the beginning. Jeremiah said it best when he said, "ask for the old paths, where the good way is, and walk in it; then you will find rest for your souls" (Jer. 6:16).

What is America's greatest need? Don't blame politicians for the moral collapse. Don't point the finger at the education system. All these are simply fruits of a root problem. We have a generation in America that does not know Christ primarily because the church has not made Him known. What is our greatest need? It is found in II Chronicles 34. The Church of Jesus Christ needs to find the Book of God in the house of God and take it to the king!

I have tremendous hope in the future of America. I believe we could very well be on the threshold of another genuine spiritual awakening in our land. Could it be that as in the days of Josiah, God is about to give us a reprieve, a revival if you please, before He returns? Do you remember the parable of the unjust judge that is recorded for all posterity in Luke 18? A widow came to him for justice and got none. This was a judge who "did not fear God, nor regard man," and did not fear this woman. But she didn't sit still. She kept coming to his door. Knock, knock, knock, but he didn't open the door. He did not fear God. He did not fear man, and he did not fear this woman. She came again. Knock, knock, knock. But he did not open because he did not fear God, nor man, nor this woman. She continued to knock, but he did not open because he did not fear God, nor man, nor this woman. She kept on knocking, and finally he opened the door. At this point the Lord Jesus said, "How much more will your heavenly Father open the door to you if you keep petitioning Him?" Then He said, "Men ought always to pray and not lose heart." Don't give up on America. Keep on praying, and keep on knocking!

Building Fund Day:
For such a time as this

I Chronicles 29:1-20

As a pastor I have had the unique privilege of serving two churches which have had long and illustrative histories, the First Baptist Church of Fort Lauderdale, Florida, and the First Baptist Church of Dallas, Texas. Time and again our spiritual forefathers have risen to the occasion when the hour of need has come. Down through history those before us have sacrificed and served that we might enjoy the benefits of their labor. We are deeply indebted to them. Our children have had the opportunity to be saved and grow up in the faith of God through these ministries because so many sacrificed so much in years gone by. Now, the baton has passed to us. We must do the same for the 21st century! May our children and grandchildren look back upon us and remember us as a people of faith. We have come to the kingdom "for such a time as this."

One of the most informative, instructional, and inspirational passages in all of Scripture is found in the twenty-eighth and twenty-ninth chapters of the first book of

Chronicles. David and his people were confronted with a challenge similar to the one facing those of us who are expanding church buildings. The time had come to build the temple in Jerusalem. It was to be the physical edifice where God would meet his people. After all the years in Egyptian bondage, after all the years of wilderness wanderings, after all the years of conquering Canaan, through the times of Judges and the reign of Saul and David, at last the glorious moment for the building of the temple had come. King David seized the opportunity to raise the money for the building of the magnificent edifice where Jehovah God would meet with His people for centuries to come.

David knew his whole life had been meant for that one special moment. What if you knew your whole life was meant for one special moment? What if you knew that all of your life God had prepared you to give and to prepare "for such a time as this." Like Esther who would come after him, David had come to his kingdom "for such a time as this." No wonder it was so easy to lead his people to give the necessary funds for the construction of the temple. It was the opportunity and moment of a lifetime, and God's hand was upon him.

How did the Israelites do it? How did they raise such a vast sum of money for the building of the temple? They followed seven vital principles to victory. How can we do it as a family of faith? The answer is found in the pattern and principles left for us by the ancient Israelites. They left us some scriptural guidelines for supernatural giving "for such a time as this." These guidelines have to do with the occasion of our giving, the order of our giving, the origin of our giving, the object of our giving, the opportunity of our giving, the objective of our giving, and the outcome of our giving.

The occasion of our giving

 "…the temple is not for man but for the Lord God" (I Chr. 29:1).

"Furthermore King David said to all the assembly: 'My son Solomon, whom alone God has chosen, is young and inexperienced; and the work is great, because the temple is not for man but for the Lord God'" (I Chr. 29:1).

Was the building of this magnificent temple something David thought up himself? Was it the brainchild of his constituency? No, a thousand times no! The occasion of their giving was God-caused. God had initiated the need of the temple and God had given David the plan for building it.

Consider the following Scriptures: "And the plans for all that he had by the Spirit, of the courts of the house of the Lord, of all the chambers all around, of the treasuries of the house of God, and of the treasuries for the dedicated things" (I Chr. 28:12). "All this," said David, "the Lord made me understand in writing, by *His* hand upon me, all the works of these plans" (I Chr. 28:19). "And David said to his son Solomon, 'Be strong and of good courage, and do it; do not fear nor be dismayed, for the Lord God — my God — will be with you. He will not leave you nor forsake you, until you have finished all the work for the service of the house of the Lord'" (I Chr. 28:20).

God had caused the need and God had given David the plan for carrying it out. The temple was not the imagination of a man's mind. It was initiated and orchestrated by God himself. The occasion of the Israelites giving was God-caused and God-directed.

David placed before his people the greatness of the task. He said, *"The work is great"* (I Chr. 29:1). People then and people now want to be a part of something that is great for God! Yes, the task is great for us. Do you know why some people in some churches never give of their resources willingly and joyfully? They do not believe the work is great. For some of them it has become a mere ecclesiastical ritual to be performed on Sunday morning so they might see themselves as respectable.

When we built a new church plant in Fort Lauderdale I asked our people some questions. Do you think what God is doing through our First Baptist Church is important? Do you think it is a great work? Do you think it is not for man but for God? If so, you realize the occasion of our giving like the Israelites is God-initiated and not man-initiated. David gives us the true reason why the work was great. Why? Because "the temple is not for man but for the Lord God" (I Chr. 29:1). This is why we were involved in that great work in Fort Lauderdale. It was not for us; it was for a testimony to God. Into the 21st century and long after every one of us is in heaven, people by the tens of thousands will pass those facilities and see that there was a people of faith who responded to a God-caused need who rose to the occasion of raising up a cross in the heart of a hell-bent, sinful city. The work is great! Why? Because "the temple is not for man but for the Lord God."

What is the occasion of our giving? God's blessings

brought about our needs. We were a God-blessed people. We would not need new facilities if we were a dead church. We would not need new facilities if we did not sense the urgency of the hour in reaching masses of men and women for Christ. We would not need new facilities if we existed solely for those who are here now, instead of those who are yet without our walls. We would not need new facilities if we had no vision. The truth is, we did not create the need. God did! The need before us was an invitation from God for each of us to discover how wonderfully He can provide.

The building of new facilities did not originate with us. We did everything we could for ten years to keep reaching people for Christ without constructing buildings. When one Sunday School was full we started another, then a third. When one worship service was full we started a second, and then a third. God's blessings and the impression of His Spirit upon our hearts brought about our needs. And since God's former blessings brought about our need, we could be sure that God's future blessings would be sufficient to meet the needs the former blessings caused!

What is the occasion of our giving? Like the Israelites, God has taken the initiative. The occasion of our giving is God-directed and God-initiated. This is an important principle to victory.

The order of our giving

 "...I have given to the house of my God...my own special treasure...Then the leaders...the captains...

with the officers over the kings' work, offered will-
ingly" (I Chr. 29:2-9).

"Now for the house of my God I have prepared with all my might: gold for things to be made of gold, silver for things of silver, bronze for things of bronze, iron for things of iron, wood for things of wood, onyx stones, stones to be set, glistening stones of various colors, all kinds of precious stones, and marble slabs in abundance. Moreover, because I have set my affection on the house of my God, I have given to the house of my God, over and above all that I have prepared for the holy house, my own special treasure of gold and silver: three thousand talents of gold, of the gold of Ophir, and seven thousand talents of refined silver, to overlay the walls of the houses; the gold for things of gold and the silver for things of silver, and for all kinds of work to be done by the hands of craftsmen. Who then is willing to consecrate himself this day to the Lord? Then... the leaders of the tribes of Israel, the captains of thousands and of hundreds, with the officers over the king's work, offered willingly. They gave for the work of the house of God five thousand talents and ten thousand darics of gold, ten thousand talents of silver, eighteen thousand talents of bronze, and one hundred thousand talents of iron. And whoever had precious stones gave them to the treasury of the house of the Lord, into the hand of Jehiel the Gershonite. Then the people rejoiced, for they had offered willingly, because with a loyal heart they had offered willingly to the Lord; and King David also rejoiced greatly" (I Chr. 29:2-9).

The proper order of our giving is a vital principle to victory. Note who led the way in giving. The people? No. The leadership? No. David himself, the leader. David said, "I have given my own special treasure of gold and silver" (I Chr. 29:3). David told his people what he and his family were going to do. He was giving out of his personal treasures. Some men are used to doing things out of expense accounts. David did not take money out of the government treasury to meet a need. He gave of his own personal treasures. It is interesting that David told them exactly what he and his family were going to do. He let them know he was giving one hundred twelve and a half tons of gold and two hundred sixty-two and a half tons of silver. What led David to give so liberally and sacrificially? He had "set his affection upon the house of his God." He had devoted his heart to it.

David did not simply give his personal time. There are a lot of leaders who do that. Nor did David simply give of his personal talent. Still other leaders do this. David gave of his personal treasure for the construction of the temple and it was over and above his regular giving. Note the order of the giving. First, David gave. Then the leadership gave. Then the people gave.

Examples are vitally important. Here we see David setting the example. He is practicing what Gideon preached when he said to his men, "Do as I do." It is the same principle Paul would use later when he wrote to the Philippians and said, "The things which you learned and received and heard and saw in me, these do, and the God of peace will be with you" (Phil. 4:9). It was the same principle Paul used when he wrote the Corinthian church saying, "Imitate me, just as I also imitate Christ" (I Cor. 11:1).

David made a sacrifice. Earlier he had said, "Nor will I offer burnt offerings to the Lord my God with that which costs me nothing" (II Sam. 24:24). David did not say, "Well, God, I am a very wealthy man. I'll give you out of my abundance. Here is a little token, a little tip. You know what the market has been lately. The elections are right around the corner. The economy is so unsettled. Interest rates are still quite questionable." No, David didn't say these things. He led by example. He gave a sacrificial gift out of his personal treasury.

As a pastor I wrestled with this. On the surface it appears to be that the Scripture is in contradiction. David specifically tells the people the amount of his personal gift, and yet I remember that Jesus said on the Sermon on the Mount that we should not let one hand know what our other hand is doing. There are many that are quick to point to these words of Jesus in the Sermon on the Mount. Is the Scripture in conflict? Was David out of line here? Let's note carefully the words Jesus preached on the grassy hillside in Galilee:

"Take heed that you do not do your charitable deeds before men, to be seen by them. Otherwise you have no reward from your Father in heaven. Therefore, when you do a charitable deed, do not sound a trumpet before you as the hypocrites do in the synagogues and in the streets, that they may have glory from men. Assuredly, I say to you, they have their reward. But when you do a charitable deed, do not let your left hand know what your right hand is doing, that your charitable deed may be in secret; and your Father who sees in secret will Himself reward you openly. And when you pray, you shall not be like the hypocrites. For they love to pray standing in the synagogues and on the corners of the streets, that they may be seen by men. Assuredly, I say to you, they have their reward. But you, when you pray, go into your room, and when you have shut your door, pray to your Father who is in the secret place; and your Father who sees in secret will reward you openly. And when you pray, do not use vain repetitions as the heathen do. For they think that they will be heard for their many words. Therefore do not be like them. For your Father knows the things you have need of before you ask Him" (Matt. 6:1-8).

Does Jesus mean that all giving is to be done in secret? If so, in the context, it must mean that all praying is to be done in secret. We know this is certainly not the case because as we read the Gospels we find the Lord Jesus praying publicly on almost every page and three times from the cross itself! The key to understanding this passage is to note the type of giving Jesus was discussing in the Sermon on the Mount. It was "giving to the needy." The King James Version translates it "alms." This was the specific type of giving which Jesus was referring to that should be done in secret. He was reacting to the custom of the blowing of the trumpets when a rich man would walk through the lines of poor beggars and toss in a few coins. The Lord Jesus was not referring to all giving here any more than he was referring to all praying being done in secret in the same context. What are we saying? David was right in doing what he did because his motives and his heart were pure.

David was setting the example for his people as a leader should do. When the people found out that he was committed, they gave willingly. That puts the pastor on the spot, doesn't it? When we led our churches in major giving programs our family prayed much about what we would do with our personal treasures. Like King David, we shared with our people what God led us to do. It is the price of leadership. And, we have never once been able to outgive Him. We have seen the truth and the proof of Luke 6:38 over and over again. It says, "Give, and it will be given to you: good measure, pressed down, shaken together, and running over will be put into your bosom. For with the same measure that you use, it will be measured back to you." Like David, we find great joy in giving. What is the order of our giving? The very word "leader" implies paving the way not just with time and talent, but also with treasure.

An interesting thing happens next. David did not simply give his testimony, sit down, and leave it at that. He challenged his people. He was not afraid to ask his people to join him in giving. As soon as he told them what he was going to do, he asked this question, "Who then is willing to consecrate himself this day to the Lord?" (I Chr. 29:5).

The result of David's challenge was overwhelming. The people gave "willingly." The Bible records, "Then the people rejoiced, for they had offered willingly, because with a loyal heart they had offered willingly to the Lord; and King David also rejoiced greatly" (I Chr. 29:9). They rejoiced at their leader's sacrifice and they rose to meet the challenge. The people of God always rise to meet a God-caused challenge!

It is important to note that David did not ask the others to do anything that he had not done himself. He led the way by example. He didn't say, "I'll leave it to the princes and people to come up with the necessary funds for the construction of the temple. I'll give my time and my talent but I'll let the rich people do the rest." No! David led by example. He said, "Now for the house of my God I have prepared with all my might" (I Chr. 29:2). Then he challenged the people, "Who then is willing to consecrate himself this day to the Lord?" (I Chr. 29:5). The first words of the very next verse speak volumes, "Then the leaders of the fathers' houses, leaders of the tribes of Israel, the captains of thousands and of hundreds, with the officers over the king's work, offered willingly" (I Chr. 29:6).

It is a probing question, "Who is willing to consecrate himself today to the Lord?" At least five critical questions arise out of this verse. WHO? This is the real probing question. Will you? WHAT? What is it that David is challenging the people to do? He is challenging them to consecrate themselves to God. There is an important order to follow here. They were first to give themselves. Then they were to give of their treasure. This is the way the Macedonians gave and were commended for all posterity by the apostle Paul. He said of them, 'That in a great trial of affliction the abundance of their joy and their deep poverty abounded in the riches of their liberality" (II Cor. 8:2). He went on to say, "He who gathered much had nothing left over, and he who gathered little had no lack" (II Cor. 8:15). HOW? This is another important question arising out of verse five. That is, how were they to give? The answer is "willingly." This was a call for voluntary, self-sacrificing service. Nothing is gained for the glory of God until our hearts are willing. WHEN? When were they to consecrate themselves to God? Today! The need is urgent! Today is not too early. Tomorrow may be too late. The time is now "for such a time as this." TO WHOM? The final question of verse five is an important one. To whom are we to give? Are we to give to the church? Are we to give to the new buildings? No! We are to give to the Lord! Here is our highest service produced by a noble motive. "Who is willing to consecrate himself today to the Lord?" The people picked up the challenge of David and they gave "willingly." The Bible records, "I know also, my God, that You test the heart and have pleasure in uprightness. As for me, in the uprightness of my heart I have willingly offered all these things; and now with joy I have seen Your people, who are present here to offer willingly to you" (I Chr. 29:17). The offering received by the Israelites was a free will offering. No one told anyone else what to give. David did not tell the leaders or the people what to give. He did not assess anyone a certain amount. David simply told the people what he and his family were going to do and challenged them to meet God and do what God impressed upon their hearts.

I have a word for this. I call it grace giving. There is a kind of giving which one might call "guilt giving." It says, "I will give because I ought to give." There is also "grudge giving." It says, "I will give because I have to give." But neither of these are seen in the fund raising program of the temple. What is seen here is what we desire. It is "grace giving" which says, "I will give willingly because I want to give."

When God's order for giving is carried out it results in great rejoicing. It is not surprising that those who have no real joy or rejoicing are usually those who are selfish and stingy. The Israelites were so full of joy one would think they must have just received some tremendous gift. After all, most people find joy in getting! But here we see an amazing principle. Their joy was from giving and not from getting. The world says joy comes from getting. We who know Christ know better. The Word says real joy comes from giving. David and his people discovered the truth that "it is more blessed to give than to receive" (Acts 20:35).

What was the outcome of it all? The giving became contagious. First David gave, then the leaders gave, then all Israel got in on it and gave willingly. David said, "Now with joy I have seen Your people, who are present here to offer willingly to You" (I Chr. 29:17).

The occasion of our giving is God-caused. The order of our giving is first the leader, then the leadership, then the people. I sense what was in David's heart when he said, "Nor will I offer burnt offerings to the Lord my God with that which costs me nothing" (II Sam. 24:24). My continual prayer is that it might be said of us what was said of the Israelites, "Then the people rejoiced, for they had offered willingly, because with a loyal heart they had offered willingly to the Lord; and King David also rejoiced greatly" (I Chr. 29:9).

The origin of our giving

 "For all things come from You, and of Your own we have given You" (I Chr. 29:14).

"But who am I, and who are my people, that we should be able to offer so willingly as this? For all things come from You, and of Your own we have given You. For we are aliens and pilgrims before You, as were all our fathers; our days on earth are as a shadow, and without hope. O Lord our God, all this abundance that we have prepared to build You a house for Your holy name is from Your hand, and is all Your own" (I Chr. 29: 14-16).

Where do we find the origin of our giving? How can we possibly give what God has impressed upon our hearts? Where is the origin of our giving? Many are quick to look into the bank account balances. Others look to the origin of their giving in stock portfolios or life insurance policies or the like. What is the origin of our giving? David discovered it! He said, "For all things come from You, and of Your own we have given You" (I Chr. 29:14). This is what the songwriter meant when he said, "All I have needed Thy hand has provided; great is Thy faithfulness, Lord unto me" (by Thomas O. Chisholm).

As a pastor, I often felt in my own heart what David surely felt when he said, "Who am I, and who are my people, that we should be able to offer so willingly as this?" (I Chr. 29:14). How can this possibly come about? The secret is in the last phrase in verse 14. Listen to it. Don't miss it. Here is the key for our personal stewardship. "For all things come from You, and of Your own we have given You" (I Chr. 29:14).

Do you see it? Everything belongs to God. We are not to give out of our limited resources, but we are privileged to give out of God's unlimited resources. It all comes from God and we have the ability to "give out of God's hand." God owns all the wealth in this world and the next. David said it this way, "For all that is in heaven and in earth is Yours" (I Chr. 29:11). In the Psalms he declared, "The earth is the Lord's, and all its fullness" (Ps. 24:1). Paul put it this way, "For of Him and through Him and to Him are all things, to whom be glory forever" (Rom. 11:36). Yes, God owns all the wealth in this world and the next. Not only does God own everything, God wants his wealth in circulation. We learn this from the familiar passage from Malachi which said, "Bring all the tithes into the storehouse, that there may be food in My house, and try Me now in this, says the Lord of hosts, if I will not open for you the windows of heaven and pour out for you such blessing that there will not be room enough to receive it" (Mal. 3:10). In God's economy the earth had one theme in the beginning. It was give — give — give — give. The sun gave. The earth gave. The animals gave. Man gave. The trees gave. The enemy then introduced a new concept and it was get — get — get — get. And man became greedy and began to live by this philosophy. However, God wants his wealth in circulation.

Think this through. God owns it all and wants it in circulation. Here is another important point. All God's wealth belongs to His children. Listen to Paul, "And if children, then heirs — heirs of God and joint heirs with Christ, if indeed we suffer with Him, that we may also be glorified together" (Rom. 8:17). We are heirs of God. It all belongs to us. You say if we are heirs then where are our riches? How do we lay hold on what is ours from God? Now, if God owns it all, wants it in circulation, and it belongs to us…how do we get in on it? The way to appropriate God's wealth is to give. This is what Jesus is trying to get us to see when He said, "Give, and it will be given to you: good measure, pressed down, shaken together, and running over will be put into your bosom. For with the same measure that you use, it will be measured back to you" (Luke

6:38). We are to give out of God's resources, not our own. David put it this way, "Give out of God's hand." We are not necessarily to give what we think we can afford, but we are to reach over into His abundant and unlimited resources and give from them. What a privilege. The issue is not what do I have the ability to do. That philosophy is giving out of my own hand and God gets no glory in that. The issue is what has God said that He desires to do through me? What is it that He desires for me to believe by faith to give from His hand? What are we saying? Everything comes from God! He is the origin of our giving. David said it well when he said, "For all things come from You, and of Your own we have given You" (I Chr. 29:14).

Everything comes from God. This is what David is reminding his people when he says, "For we are aliens and pilgrims before You...our days on earth are as a shadow" (I Chr. 29:15). Life is short — too short. Our days are like a shadow. We only pass this way once. We are merely stewards along this journey. The question is, "What have you done with that which God has entrusted with you?" Some of my readers have no time to lose. Some of you have hair that is graying and may find this to be the last great opportunity in your entire lifetime to do something big for God.

The way is before us "for such a time as this". The occasion of our giving is God-caused. The order of our giving is first the heart and then the personal treasure. The origin of our giving is in God Himself. We are not to give from our own limited resources but out of His hand from His unlimited resources. "Everything comes from God."

The object of our giving

 "...with joy I have seen Your people, who are present here to offer willingly to You" (I Chr. 29.17).

"I know also, my God, that You test the heart and have pleasure in uprightness. As for me, in the uprightness of my heart I have willingly offered all these things; and now with joy I have seen Your people, who are present here to offer willingly to You" (I Chr. 29:17).

To what or to whom are we being challenged to give? Were the Israelites giving their personal treasures to the temple? Are we giving our personal treasures to the church? Are we giving our personal treasures to brick, or mortar, or buildings? What is the object of our giving? Note carefully what David says, "...with joy I have seen Your people, who are present here to offer willingly to You" (I Chr. 29:17).

One might say, "I thought they were giving to the temple." To whom were they giving? They were giving to God. They were not giving to the temple. To whom are we giving? What is the object of our giving? We are giving to God. We are not giving to new buildings or to our church. When we put a handle on this vital principle, it will be a breakthrough for us as it was for the Israelites. The object of our giving is the Lord Jesus Himself. We simply happen to be giving through our local churches to Him.

As much as I love my church, my family and I are not giving our personal treasures to the church. We are not giving one dime to concrete or steel or mortar or concrete block or tile or carpet or pews. The object of our giving is the Lord Himself. It just happens to be that we are giving to Him through a great soul-saving station. As we take from His hand, we put it back into His other hand. And He has a way of seeing that He can trust us and when He does, He gives, and gives, and gives again. The object of our giving is the Lord Himself!

The opportunity of our giving

 "...in the uprightness of my heart I have willingly offered all these things..." (I Chr. 29:17-18).

"I know also, my God, that You test the heart and have pleasure in uprightness. As for me, in the uprightness of my heart I have willingly offered all these things; and now with joy I have seen Your people, who are present here to offer willingly to You. O Lord God of Abraham, Isaac, and Israel, our fathers, keep this forever in the intent of the thoughts of the heart of Your people, and fix their heart toward You" (I Chr. 29:17-18).

How does a Christian walk in "uprightness?" He does so by doing what he claims to be. A Christian walks in integrity when his walk matches his talk and when his life matches his lips. We say we are a people of faith. We say we live by faith. David reminds us that "God tests the heart and has pleasure in uprightness" (I Chr. 29:17). Yes, God tests our hearts to see if we really dare to live by faith. The Bible admonishes us, "As you therefore have received Christ Jesus the Lord, so walk in Him" (Col. 2:6). Many are quick to say we are saved by faith. But so few of us continue in the same way. We say we are saved by faith, but we live our life by works. If faith is good enough to save us it is surely good enough to live by. So many Christians who walk through the door of Christ by faith revert to what they can see and do themselves in living the Christian life. God is testing the integrity of our hearts.

What is the opportunity of our giving? The opportunity before us is to please God by living by faith. He is "pleased with integrity." Some of us pride ourselves in our own integrity and need to hear these words and heed them. We say that we are a Christian by faith alone in Jesus Christ. We say we believe God will never leave us. We say we believe all of His promises. And yet so many of us live by sight. Our hope is in our savings accounts or stock portfolios or real estate holdings or retirement packages. This is a call for integrity in Christian living. David put it this way, "I know also, my God, that You test the heart and have pleasure in uprightness" (I Chr. 29:17). What an opportunity is ours to say to the world, "All things are possible — only believe!"

Now, this creates a great deal of pressure upon an individual. However, the pressure is put upon us by the Holy Spirit Himself. When we gave to build the new buildings in Fort Lauderdale we made a faith pledge to God that was given weekly and systematically over three years. Many of us have spent a lifetime doing that with the world. We have done such things as sign 30-year mortgages with a lending institution and promise to pay on the first of the month for the next 30 years.

Is there a Biblical basis for a faith pledge? Indeed there is. Do you remember when Paul wrote to the church at Corinth and challenged them to make a gift? Listen to his own words, "Now concerning the collection for the saints, as I have given orders to the churches of Galatia, so you must do also: On the first day of the week let each one of you lay something aside, storing up as he may prosper, that there be no collections when I come. And when I come, whomever you approve by your letters I will send to bear your gift to Jerusalem. But if it is fitting that I go also, they will go with me" (I Cor. 16:1-4).

One year later Paul writes back to the same church (recorded in II Corinthians, 8-9) and says to them that he is sending Titus to make sure the gift is ready when he gets there. Note carefully what Paul says, "So let each one give as he purposes in his heart, not grudgingly or of necessity; for God loves a cheerful giver" (II Cor. 9:7). The New International Version translates that Scripture "That which you decided in your heart to give." In the original language the word is "prohaire-omai." It means "to decide ahead of time to do a certain thing." The Corinthians had made a faith-pledge ahead of time and they gave it when the time came.

We did exactly the same thing Paul admonished this first century church to do. We decided ahead of time what we were going to give from God's hand to the Lord over the next three years. We were challenged to make a gift just as Paul challenged the church in I Corinthians Chapter 16. Over the next three years we gave what we decided "ahead of time" to give. We called it a faith-pledge. It doesn't really matter what you call it as long as you meet God and give from His hand.

We are now at the heart of the issue before us. We are dealing with God Himself who knows our hearts. In a very real sense our own spiritual integrity is revealed at this point. It is no wonder some feel pressure from the Holy Spirit. We call it a faith pledge because the issue is our faith in God's ability to provide. The issue is not our faith in what the economy is going to do or who the next president of United States will be, nor anything else that man can do, manipulate, or orchestrate. The opportunity before us is our faith to believe in God's reachness and willingness to provide through us from His hand for His work. What an opportunity! We have the opportunity in our giving to show the world that Jesus Christ is alive and at work in and through us to the Father's glory.

Our integrity and our motives are at issue here. Do you know that it is possible for a Christian to do something that in the eyes of man is wonderful but in the eyes of God is detestable? There are a lot of folks who do things in the eyes of men that are wonderful. But Jesus put it this way, "No one can serve two masters; for either he will hate the one and love the other, or else he will be loyal to the one and despise the other. You cannot serve God and mammon" (Matt. 6:24). Now the Pharisees, who were lovers of money, also heard all these things, and they derided Him. And He said to them, "You are those who justify yourselves before men, but God knows your hearts. For what is highly esteemed among men is an abomination in the sight of God" (Luke 16:13-15). David said the same thing in the following way, "I know also, my God, that You test the heart and have pleasure in uprightness. As for me, in the uprightness of my heart I have willingly offered all these things; and now with joy I have seen Your people, who are present here to offer willingly to You" (I Chr. 29:17).

As commendable as David's efforts were and as valuable as his gifts were, had his motives been the applause of men the whole matter would have been an abomination to God and detestable before His eyes. David sought to walk by faith in integrity and to glorify God in the process. We catch a glimpse of his heart when he says, "O Lord God of Abraham, Isaac, and Israel, our fathers, keep this forever in the intent of the thoughts of the heart of Your people, and fix their heart toward You" (I Chr. 29:18). David desired for it to become a lifestyle, not only for himself, but for his people. It will become a lifestyle for us as we keep our hearts loyal to Him. David's concern was that his people continue and that his pattern of giving not just become a one-time shot, but a transformation of a lifestyle toward faith and dependence upon God forever.

Our personal giving is the place where our spiritual integrity is revealed before God. God is measuring our personal integrity. David said the task was great because the temple was "not for man but for the Lord God" (I Chr. 29:1). May it be said of us what was said of the church at Rome, "First, I thank my God through Jesus Christ for you all, that your faith is spoken of throughout the whole world" (Rom. 1:8). What an opportunity we have to be a blessing and encouragement to the work of God around the world.

The objective of our giving

 "...so all the assembly blessed the Lord ..." (I Chr. 29:20).

"But who am I, and who are my people, that we should be able to offer so willingly as this? For all things come from You, and of Your own we have given You" (I Chr. 29:14).

"I know also, my God, that You test the heart and have pleasure in uprightness. As for me, in the uprightness of my heart I have willingly offered all these things; and now with joy I have seen Your people, who are present here to offer willingly to You" (I Chr. 29:17).

"Then David said to all the assembly, "Now bless the Lord Your God." So all the assembly blessed the Lord God of their fathers, and bowed their heads and prostrated themselves before the Lord and the king" (I Chr. 29:20)

What is the objective in giving? Our objective is that everyone become involved. Our objective is that everyone prays and everyone fasts and everyone meets God and everyone gives from God's hand. The Israelites victory won the day because each one did his or her part. The one thing that stands out in each of the above passages of Scripture from Chronicles is that each one of the Israelites was involved. It was a case of total participation.

The early church had the same objective and followed the Israelites example. "When the Day of Pentecost had fully come, they were all with one accord in one place" (Acts 2:1). "Now all who believed were together, and had all things in common, and sold their possessions and goods, and divided them among all, as anyone had need" (Acts 2:44-45). "Now the multitude of those who believed were of one heart and one soul; neither did anyone say that any of the things he possessed was his own, but they had all things in common. And with great power the apostles gave witness to the resurrection of the Lord Jesus. And great grace was upon them all. Nor was there anyone among them who lacked; for all who were possessors of lands or houses sold them, and brought the proceeds of the things that were sold, and laid them at the apostles' feet; and they distributed to each as anyone had need" (Acts 4:32-35).

Our objective in giving is the same. We long to see everyone involved with no one missing the blessing of giving. Someone might say, "I have no money; I have nothing to give." Then give from God's hand. Proverbs 13:23 reminds us, "Much food is in the fallow ground of the poor." Fallow ground is ground that has not been used, plowed, nor planted for a considerable period of time. God is saying there are resources available where we think there are none. There is much food in the fallow ground of the poor! God show us fallow ground!

Everyone gave to the Lord for the building of the temple. Old men gave. Young men gave. Middle-aged men gave. Women gave. Young couples gave. Singles gave. Teenagers and boys and girls gave. Those without money sold their possessions and gave them. It was victory day because everyone got in on it.

Remember, the occasion of our offering is God-caused. The order of our offering is first from the heart and then from our gifts. The origin of our offering is to give from God's hand. The object of our offering is the Lord Himself. The opportunity of our offering is to please God by being people of faith. The objective is everyone being involved.

The outcome of our giving

 Yours, O Lord, is the greatness, the power and the glory, the victory and the majesty..."
(I Chr. 29:10-13).

"Therefore David blessed the Lord before all the assembly; and David said: "Blessed are You, Lord God of Israel, our Father, forever and ever. Yours, O Lord, is the greatness, the power and the glory, the victory and the majesty; for all that is in heaven and in earth is Yours; Yours is the kingdom, O Lord, and You are exalted as head over all. Both riches and honor come from You, and You reign over all. In Your hand is power and might; in Your hand it is to make great and to give strength to all. Now therefore, our God, we thank You and praise Your glorious name" (I Chr. 29:10-13).

"'I know also, my God, that You test the heart and have pleasure in uprightness. As for me, in the uprightness of my heart I have willingly offered all these things; and now with joy I have seen Your people, who are present here to offer willingly to You. O Lord God of Abraham, Isaac, and Israel, our fathers, keep this forever in the intent of the thoughts of the heart of Your people, and fix their heart toward You. And give my son Solomon a loyal heart to keep Your commandments and Your testimonies and Your statutes, to do all these things, and to build the temple for which I have made provision.' Then David said to all the assembly, 'Now bless the Lord your God.' So all the assembly blessed the Lord God of their fathers, and bowed their heads and prostrated themselves before the Lord and the king" (I Chr. 29:20).

What was the outcome of the Israelites giving? God got the glory! The people pointed to His greatness and not that of David or the leadership. The outcome of their giving was all praise going to the Lord God. Can you imagine their joy when the offering was taken? Can you just see David standing up in front of his people saying "Blessed are You, Lord God of Israel, our Father, forever and ever. Yours, O Lord, is the greatness, the power and the glory, the victory and the majesty; for all that is in heaven and in earth is Yours; Yours is the kingdom, O Lord, and You are exalted as head over all. Both riches and honor come from You, and You reign over all. In Your hand is power and might; In Your hand it is to make great and to give strength to all. Now therefore, our God, we thank You and praise Your glorious name" (I Chr. 29: 10-13). God was glorified that day because where a man puts his treasure his heart is sure to follow. They "bowed their heads and prostrated themselves before the Lord and the king" (I Chr. 29:20).

Their giving resulted in revival. Why is this? So often greed is one of the major obstacles to revival. Usually, in the end, money is the last thing to which people hold. There are a lot of people who give their time. There are a lot of people who give their talents but so many hold back their personal treasures. These men and women said, "God, it's all yours; here it is!" And Jesus said, "For where your treasure is, there your heart will be also" (Matt. 6:21). Our hearts always follow our treasures. If we primarily put our treasures in some kind of activity, our hearts will be there. If we put our treasures in the work of God, our hearts will be there. And revival will result! The Israelites made a sacrifice for those who would come after them. They gave to the Lord God…for others and not for themselves.

One might think that such incredible success as David and his people saw would make them burst with pride. Quite the contrary, it brought a deep sense of gratitude and a humble spirit. "David said to the whole assembly…'Look what we have done!'" No! That's not what he said. He said, "'Now bless the Lord your God.' So all the assembly blessed the Lord God of their fathers, and bowed their heads and prostrated themselves before the Lord and the king" (I Chr. 29:20). What an outcome there was of praise and worship. Oh that we might join them in bringing great honor and glory to the living Christ "for such a time as this."

The task before the 21st century church is great. We are a part of something grand and glorious because what we are about is "not for man but for the Lord God." How can we do it? We can follow the example of the Israelites and these scriptural guidelines for supernatural giving:

(1) *The occasion of our giving.* The occasion of our giving is God-caused. Ours is a God-caused need. Remember, if God's former blessings brought about our present needs, his future blessings will be sufficient to meet the needs the former blessings have caused! We can trust the Lord. He is the initiator of our need.

(2) *The order of our giving.* The pastor and leadership must lead the way and the people will follow. First we are to give ourselves and then our gifts. May we be able to join the Israelites and may it be said of us, "The people rejoiced, for they had offered willingly, because with a loyal heart they had offered willingly to the Lord; and King David also rejoiced greatly" (I Chr. 29:9).

(3) *The origin of our giving.* Our ability to give comes from God. "Everything comes from God and we have given only what comes from His hand." He owns it all, wants his wealth in circulation. We are his heirs, and the way to appropriate his wealth is to give! He is the origin of our giving.

(4) *The object of our giving.* We are not giving to brick, nor mortar, nor our church, but the object of our giving is to

the Lord Himself. David put it this way, "Now with joy I have seen Your people, who are present here to offer willingly to You" (I Chr. 29:17).

(5) *The opportunity of our giving.* We have the opportunity to be a tremendous witness for Christ by walking by faith. God knows our hearts. Integrity is the by-word. We say we are a people of faith and now it is time to let our walk match our talk and our life match our lips. Like David, we too know that God "tests the heart and has pleasure in uprightness" (I Chr. 29:17).

(6) *The objective of our giving.* The objective of our giving is that everyone meet God and give by revelation. Everyone being involved is the key to victory. No one is unimportant. Remember there is much food in the fallow ground of the poor.

(7) *The outcome of our giving.* The ultimate outcome of it all is that the Lord Jesus Christ might be glorified and honored and praised. Our desire is that we praise the Lord our God and give Him glory through the whole experience.

Farewell to the Church Day

Acts 20:17-21:1

One of the most emotionally challenging experiences in the life of a pastor is saying goodbye to a people he has loved, to a church he has served as under-shepherd, as he and his family embark upon a new field of service. In my own personal experience, this has happened four times and each experience produced its own unique and memorable expressions.

The call of God to a new field of service is a mysterious thing. Those who say it is easy haven't done it. What does a pastor say when he leaves a people and a pulpit he loves for a ministry elsewhere? Does he spend time talking about the past, what we were? Does he talk about the present, what we are? Does he talk about the potential, what we can become? Does he simply ignore the emotion of the moment? There is a beautiful biblical pattern which every pastor can follow. The great Apostle Paul pastored the church at Ephesus for over three years. There came the time for him to follow God's call away from Ephesus to a more expanded ministry. What would he say to these men and women he loved so dearly and who had supported him? What would he say to those who stood with him against such incredible odds? The 20th chapter of Acts holds the answer.

My wife Susie and I visited the ancient city of Ephesus in modern day Turkey shortly before we resigned our pastorate for a more expanded ministry. In Paul's day there was a road that led from the city down to the sea. It was commonly referred to as "Harbor Road." We stood on that road for a moment, then sat down on a rock and read this passage from Acts 20. I would suggest that any pastor who was about to leave his church say what Paul said to the Ephesians almost two thousand years ago. We should all join him in challenging our church to look at our past, to look at our present, and to look at our potential.

Look at our past

 From Miletus he sent to Ephesus and called for the elders of the church.

And when they had come to him, he said to them: "You know, from the first day that I came to Asia, in what manner I always lived among you,

Serving the Lord with all humility, with many tears and trials which happened to me by the plotting of the Jews;

How I kept back nothing that was helpful, but proclaimed it to you, and taught you publicly and from house to house,

Testifying to Jews, and also to Greeks, repentance
toward God and faith toward our Lord Jesus Christ"
(Acts 20:17-21).

Listen to the great Apostle in these verses. He called them
to look back at their past and be reminded of how he lived
among them "serving" the Lord. As we look back over these
years together we can give thanks to God for the way we have
served together in so many ways. When Rehoboam became
king of the southern kingdom some of the elders gave him some
good advice. "And they spoke to him, saying, 'If you will be a
servant to these people today, and serve them, and answer
them, and speak good words to them, then they will be your servants forever'" (I Kin. 12:7). Although we have often failed, it
has been our aim to live with this spirit and serve one another
along the way. There have been times when we, like Paul, have
served with "humility and tears and trials." We have known as
a pastor what it is to weep over you in times of your sin, others
in times of your sorrows, and still others in times of sufferings.
Yes, in many ways this has been a time of tears.

As Paul challenged his people to look at their past he
reminded them how his message had been that of "repentance toward God and faith toward our Lord Jesus Christ"
(Acts 20:21). This is the message that is never changed from
our pulpit. That is, repentance toward God and faith in the
Lord Jesus Christ.

Paul said goodbye with a look to the past. When I left our
First Baptist Church in Dallas, I recalled what a rich past our
church had enjoyed. We had a solid foundation upon which

to build that stood upon a century-old heritage of only two pastors, the great George W. Truett and the incomparable W. A. Criswell. This was a great asset which kept us tethered to the cross and to the word of God.

Yes, we leave our church with a look to our past and say with the great Apostle Paul "I always lived among you, serving the Lord with all humility, with many tears and trials…I kept back nothing that was helpful, but proclaimed…repentance toward God and faith toward our Lord Jesus Christ" (Acts 20:18-21).

As we leave our present place of service it is not only important to look at our past but also to:

Look at our present

 How I kept back nothing that was helpful, but proclaimed it to you, and taught you publicly and from house to house,

Testifying to Jews, and also to Greeks, repentance toward God and faith toward our Lord Jesus Christ.

And see, now I go bound in the spirit to Jerusalem, not knowing the things that will happen to me there,

Except that the Holy Spirit testifies in every city, saying that chains and tribulations await me.

But none of these things move me; nor do I count my life dear to myself, so that I may finish my race with joy, and the ministry which I received from the Lord Jesus, to testify to the gospel of the grace of God.

And indeed, now I know that you all, among whom I have gone preaching the kingdom of God, will see my face no more.

Therefore I testify to you this day that I am innocent of the blood of all men.

For I have not shunned to declare to you the whole counsel of God (Acts 20:20-27).

Paul tells his people that he goes "bound" in the Spirit. This is an interesting Greek word which illustrates what it is to be "in chains" in Colossians 4:3. The same word also describes Lazarus being "wrapped" in grave clothes in John 11:44. Paul is telling his people that just as the chains bind one in prison or grave clothes bind those who are dead, so the Spirit compels Paul. He can do no other. Many of us know this feeling. Especially when he goes on to say "not knowing what might happen to me there." Paul is telling his people that there's nothing he can do about it. He is compelled. This is a God thing and is wrapped in the supernatural.

Paul is consumed with "finishing his race" (Acts 20:24). His aim is on completing the task God has given him. When our youngest daughter Holly was in high school she ran on the 400 meter relay team during track season. As I watched her receive the baton and hand it off, I was reminded that this is much the way the church has gone. In our own First Baptist Church in Dallas, George W. Truett had a long leg in the relay. He put us out in front. Then Dr. W. A. Criswell ran longer than Dr. Truett and lapped everyone in the field. Then, in a sense, we dropped the baton. Some people on our team took off the uniforms and left to join another team. Others just sat down and stopped cheering. But most remained faithful. It was my assignment in the relay to pick up the baton and seek to make up some lost ground, to catch back up and get us back in the race. Making up lost ground is a challenge, but it can be done. When my days there were concluded, I was confident in knowing that I had finished the part in the race God had called me to run and I was able to pass the baton to Dr. Mac Brunson who now is taking the church to heights it has not seen in years.

As Paul looks at the present at Ephesus he speaks of a very important principle for a ministry in verse 24. He speaks of "the ministry which I received from the Lord Jesus." Here's the essence of effective ministry. There's a difference in an achieved ministry and a received ministry. Paul speaks of "receiving" a ministry. An achieved ministry is often manipulative. An achieved ministry seeks the applause and amen of men. In some ways an achieved ministry may fail although it succeeds. A received ministry is one that seeks only the applause and amen of God. There's a sense in which a received ministry may fail in the eyes of men though it succeeds in the eyes of God. We have the ministry to which we've been called and it is one we have "received" from the Lord Jesus Christ. Paul is leaving Ephesus with a clear conscience (Acts 20:25-27). If the Ephesians failed in the future the fault would not lie with him. He had gotten them on their knees. He had trained them. He'd accomplished what God called him to do and now he was leaving without regrets.

When we bid a farewell to our church we should do so by looking at the past and remembering that we have served with humility and tears even in the midst of trials. We should also look to our present and see that God is in control and that He's not brought us out except to take us in. There's a final look. We should:

Look at our potential

 Therefore take heed to yourselves and to all the flock, among which the Holy Spirit has made you over-seers, to shepherd the church of God which He pur-chased with His own blood.

For I know this, that after my departure savage wolves will come in among you, not sparing the flock.

Also from among yourselves men will rise up, speaking perverse things, to draw away the disciples after themselves.

Therefore watch, and remember that for three years I did not cease to warn everyone night and day with tears.

So now, brethren, I commend you to God and to the word of His grace, which is able to build you up and give you an inheritance among all those who are sanctified.

I have coveted no one's silver or gold or apparel.

Yes, you yourselves know that these hands have provided for my necessities, and for those who were with me.

I have shown you in every way, by laboring like this, that you must support the weak. And remember the words of the Lord Jesus, that He said, "It is more blessed to give than to receive."

And when he had said these things, he knelt down and prayed with them all.

Then they all wept freely, and fell on Paul's neck and kissed him,

Sorrowing most of all for the words which he spoke, that they would see his face no more. And they accompanied him to the ship.

Now it came to pass, that when we had departed from them and set sail, running a straight course we came to Cos, the following day to Rhodes, and from there to Patara (Acts 20:28-38, 21:1).

Now Paul turns his attention to the future and begins to challenge his people to "take heed...keep watch...be on guard." He knew the church at Ephesus was Christ's church. Our Lord had bought it with His own blood. So we encourage our people as we leave our place of service to "be on guard" and to keep watch over themselves and the flock of God. The two personal pronouns used here are present-active imperative. That is, the job is for each person in the church and not just the deacons or church leaders.

Paul called on the leaders of the church at Ephesus to be "shepherds" (Acts 20:28) in order to care for the sheep. Somewhere out there in the councils of heaven, God has already appointed his choice for a new pastor. Whatever we do as we leave a church, we should never seek to maneuver nor orchestrate nor manipulate nor promote what we leave behind.

When Paul was first sent out to ministry from the great missionary church at Antioch, the Bible records that the church "laid hands on him and sent him away" (Acts 13:3). The next verse says that he was "sent on his way by the Holy Spirit" (Acts 13:4). Verse 3 says that the church "sent" him. Yet, verse 4 says that the Holy Spirit "sent" him. Who sent him? Who sends us? The church or the Holy Spirit? If we were reading these words written by Luke and recorded for all posterity in Acts 13 in the language in which they were written, we would be amazed at what we see. In the language of the New Testament there are two diametrically opposite words used in these two verses which we translate into the same English word "sent." In verse 3 we find the word "apoluō." Although it is translated "sent" in Acts 13:3, every other place it's used in the New Testament it's translated "to release or to let go." For example, this same word is found in Acts 3:13 when it speaks of a prisoner who's been "released" from prison. In contrast, the word in Acts 13:4 which we translate "sent" is a strong word in Greek, "ekpempō." It means to thrust out, to push out or send out. Thus, what happened was that the Holy Spirit and the church recognized and "released" him to do the work of the ministry. There is something very supernatural about the ministry of a pastor and a people. Some churches never see the blessing of God because they take it upon themselves to find a pastor much like a bank might find a president. They bring someone to the church the Holy

Spirit has never sent. There are other churches where God sends His particular person to His particular place but the church never recognizes it and never truly releases him to do the work of ministry and exercise his gift as pastor. However, when we find a church where God has sent the pastor and the church recognizes and releases him to do the work of ministry, we find the power of God and the blessing of God coming upon them. Such was the case of Paul's ministry which he had received from the Lord at Ephesus.

Paul goes on to say in his final address to the church he loved, "I have shown you in every way by laboring like this, that you must support the weak. And remember the words of the Lord Jesus, that he said 'It is more blessed to give than to receive'" (Acts 20:35). As the church was to look to the future and to view their potential, Paul challenged them to esteem each other as better than themselves. The world is watching the church. It is a wonderful opportunity to give the world a beautiful picture of what God can do through a group of men and women who are abandoned to Him. Every church has a glorious future. As we embark upon a new ministry that we've received from the Lord, we join Paul and the Ephesians in looking to our potential.

So, what can I say as a final word as pastor? I cannot improve upon Paul's words to his people so I simply say, "I commend you to God and to the word of His grace, which is able to build you up and give you an inheritance among all those that are sanctified" (Acts 20:32). What can the pastor do when he leaves? Commit his people to God and the word of His grace! Paul later wrote to another church he loved and said now abide these three things, faith, hope, love. Thus, we look to the past with love. We look to the present with faith. For without faith it is impossible to please God. And, we look to the future with hope. He is our blessed hope!

For several years I was privileged to be the pastor of the First Baptist Church in Dallas. In September of 1887 the great George W. Truett was called to be the pastor of First Baptist Church in Dallas. He began what was to be a century of two of the most God blessed pastor-preachers in all of church history. It was a high calling and a tremendous privilege to stand in that same pulpit and seek to carry the baton which they had held.

On a given day during our pastorate in Dallas I visited with Mr. A. B. Tanko who at the time was 97 years of age. He was keen and had an incredibly sharp mind. He told me about being present in the sanctuary at First Baptist the last time the great George W. Truett came to his pulpit. He was terminally ill. The devastating effects of cancer had racked his body with pain for many months. He'd been out of the pulpit for an extended time and everyone knew that this more than likely would be the last trip to the sacred desk after 47 years. Tanko described the emotion of the moment and the atmospheric expectation of the filled building.

Dr. Truett entered that morning from the choir room door walking slowly with a cane. The once stately, golden-throated orator was now bent in pain. He preached his final message and came down on the floor in front of the pulpit to issue the invitation. The choir began to sing, "He leadeth me, O blessed thought, O words with heavenly comfort fraught, what e'er I do, where e'er I be, still tis God's hand that leadeth me." The pastor stopped the invitation. An eerie silence fell over the room and he quoted the last verse of the hymn from memory and those were the last words he ever spoke in that pulpit. "And when my task on earth is done, when by God's grace the victory's won, even death's cold wave I will not flee, since God through Jordan leadeth me. He leadeth me, he leadeth me, by His own hand He leadeth me, His faithful follower I will be, for by His grace He leadeth me." (Joseph Gilmore)

And with those words Dr. Truett joined the Apostle Paul in saying, "I commend you to God and to the word of His grace, which is able to build you up and give you an inheritance among all those who are sanctified."

Deacon Ordination Sunday

Acts 6:1-7

The church of our Lord Jesus Christ is not simply a local organization, it is a living organism. It is supernatural in its function. A study of the rapid growth and divine blessing upon the early church reveals that one of their most important ingredients was love and unity among the family of faith. By the time we reach the sixth chapter of Acts the church has been exploding and thousands of people have been born into the family of God. It is at this point that God gives a gift to the local church. It is the gift of the ministry of the deacon. There's nothing in the New Testament that gives credence to what has evolved into a "board of deacons" in the modern church. The New Testament model was more of a "fellowship of deacons" whose primary function was to be servants and to maintain the unity of the fellowship in the bond of peace. The ministry of the deacon finds its roots almost 2,000 years ago in the church at Jerusalem. Note first:

Its instigation

 Now in those days, when the number of the disciples was multiplying, there arose a complaint against the Hebrews by the Hellenists, because their widows were neglected in the daily distribution.

Then the twelve summoned the multitude of the disciples and said, "It is not desirable that we should leave the word of God and serve tables" (Acts 6:1-2).

As the "number of the disciples was multiplying" there arose a problem in the church. Great numbers were being saved. Satan had tried his best to corrupt the church from without in the fourth and fifth chapters of Acts. He had seen that Peter and John were arrested, others of the Apostles met similar fates and were thrown into prison. They were placed before various tribunals, they were beaten, and they were commanded that they should not speak in the name of Jesus Christ again. But persecutions from without simply grew the church that much more. Now, as we come to Acts chapter 6 we see that Satan's modus operandi changes. Now he seeks to corrupt from within. How? Jealousy. There arose murmuring and complaining among members of the church. It is now that the ministry of the deacon is born. In fact, it was birthed out of a problem in the church.

The Hellenistic Jews were convinced that the Hebraic Jews and the Apostles were showing favoritism to each other and that they were being slighted. Jealously arose within the family of faith. The Hebraic Jews were natives of Palestine.

They were more conservative and traditional in their approach to life. The Hellenistic Jews were Greek-speaking Jews from other nations who had gathered in Jerusalem. They tended to be more cosmopolitan and more progressive. They began to complain that partiality was being shown toward their Hebraic brothers. Jealousy had raised its ugly head.

There were two primary dangers that faced the early church at this stage of its growth. One was prejudice. The Grecian Jews perceived that the Apostles were prejudiced against them. The other danger was professionalism. That is, that the preacher and leaders could be hired to do all the work. The Apostles very wisely threw the ball back into the court of the fellowship of faith. Thus, the office of the deacon was born out of a potential problem. The wisdom of the early church leaders is apparent when we read the names of those first seven deacons. Listen to their names ... Stephen, Philip, Prochorus, Nicanor, Timon, Parmenas, and Nicolas. All seven of these names are Hellenistic names. In reaching out to those who felt slighted, the Apostles appointed the first seven deacons solely from the group of Hellenistic Jews.

Thus, the ministry of the deacon finds its instigation in service. In meeting the needs of the membership. Why? In order to keep the unity of the family of faith in the bond of peace. Deacons ought to be the best at that of anyone. The primary reason for their existence is not to cause dissension but to maintain love and unity among the family of faith. This is their origin. This is the very reason the ministry of the deacon was instigated.

Its initiation

 Therefore, brethren, seek out from among you seven men of good reputation, full of the Holy Spirit and wisdom, whom we may appoint over this business (Acts 6:3).

What are the qualifications, the requirements, for initiation into the ministry of the deacon? Acts 6:3 lays them out, "therefore, brethren, seek out from among you seven men of good reputation, full of the Holy Spirit and wisdom, whom we may appoint over this business." The first qualification is that they be a believer. Note the word "brethren." In Greek it comes from a word that means "from the same womb." These were brothers in the truest sense. Born out of the same blood, the blood of the Lord Jesus Christ. This ministry of the deacon was born out of fellowship of a life based on a common origin. That is, they were to be of one heart and one mind with the Apostles. They were to be brothers in the truest sense.

Note secondly that they were to be "men." The Apostles said, "seek out from among you seven men" (Acts 6:3). Often when we read the word "men" translated in the New Testament, it is the Greek word anthropos. This is the generic word from which we get our word anthropology. It means men and women. For example, it is found in Matthew 5:16 when Jesus said, "Let your light so shine before men." Obviously, he didn't mean that we were only to be a witness to men but by using the word anthropos he meant generically men and women. However, this is not the word we find in the initiation of the deacon into the fellowship of the church. Here it is the word andras. This word means male or husband as opposed to female. These seven who served in the initial ministry of the deacon were not only to be believers but they were to be men.

Next, they were to have integrity. In the words of Acts 6:3 they were to be "of good reputation." This word comes from the word which means witness or martyr. These were to be men who could be counted on, whose life was characterized by an inner power and not an outer promotion. Integrity is rooted in private life and good reputation resulted in the witness of these good and godly men.

They were also to be "full of the Holy Spirit" (Acts 6:3). There are a lot of deacons who are believers, men, and filled with integrity who have been chosen to serve the church on the basis of social standing or scholarship, rather than spirituality. It is important that the deacon be a man who is "full of the Holy Spirit." This is the direct command of Ephesians 5:18 which is to "be filled with the Holy Spirit." The evidence of that is found in the following verses in the Ephesians 5 passage. In verse 19 there is an inward expression. The evidence is "singing and making melody in your heart to the Lord." The one who is full of the Holy Spirit will have a song in his heart. It is the inward expression of a life that's full of God's spirit. There's also an upward expression in the next verse, Ephesians 5:20. You will find him "giving thanks always for all things to God the Father in the name of our Lord Jesus Christ." He will have an attitude of gratitude. And, finally, there is an outward expression. Ephesians 5:21 finds him "submitting to one another in the fear of God." The initiation of a deacon should be for one who is a believer with integrity and who is full of the Holy Spirit.

Note also that he is to be "full of wisdom." The word is wisdom here and not knowledge. There is a world of difference. Knowledge is the accumulation of facts. Wisdom is the ability to discern between facts and apply them to points of need. We get wisdom from God. James says that if any of us lack wisdom we can "ask of God" and it will be given to us.

Thus, we find the instigation of the ministry of the deacon being born out of a problem of murmuring and complaining. The number one job of a deacon is to maintain love and unity in the family of faith. Next we find its initiation. Those who qualify as deacon are those who are men who know Christ, who are filled with integrity, and full of the Holy Spirit and wisdom.

Its integration

 Therefore, brethren, seek out from among you seven men of good reputation, full of the Holy Spirit and wisdom, whom we may appoint over this business;

But we will give ourselves continually to prayer and to the ministry of the word (Acts 6:3-4).

Here we see the beautiful expression of the church as the Apostles integrated their gifts with the gifts of the layman. They blended together to serve the church in mutual appreciation and mutual respect.

The deacon had his particular points of reference. They were appointed by the Apostles to be "over this business." The Greek word translated "business" appears 49 times in the New Testament and this is the only time that it is translated "business." The other 48 times it is translated "need." We get our word "deacon" from the word that's translated "distribution" in Acts 6:1 and the word translated "serve" in Acts 6:2. The same Greek word translates both of these words. It is the noun "diakonos." It is a compound word from two words in Greek. There is a preposition meaning "through" and a noun which means "dust". The very word means "through the dust". Its root is found in that of a foot washer, a servant who was charged with the task of washing the dust off people's feet. This word appears 30 times in the New Testament and 27 of those times it is translated "minister" or "servant." Only three times is it translated "deacon" or "deaconess." Phoebe is referred to as a deaconess which obviously means she was a servant of the Lord Jesus Christ. For those who have been initiated into the ministry of the deacon as we find the seven men in Acts 6, we see that their primary task was that of serving. They were primarily responsible for "serving tables" and distributing relief supplies to widows. They had their origins in meeting the needs of the fellowship in the spirit of a foot washer and in the spirit of service.

When the deacon performs his ministry there's a beautiful integration with that of the pastor. We note in Acts 6:4 that this freed the pastors to "give themselves continually to prayer and to the ministry of the word." This integration of the ministry of the deacon and the pastor provides a means for building great churches in the eyes of God.

The most important factor in church growth is the integration of the lay people and the ministerial staff. Every member should be a ministry. No one is unimportant. The usher and the preacher are in the same ministry. I always told our ushers in my pastorates that if an individual walked through the door and felt unwelcome or had a bad experience he would never hear a word the preacher was saying. Churches that have the blessing of God are those who are wise enough to see the integration of the ministry of the pastor and the deacon.

Its inspiration

 And the saying pleased the whole multitude. And they chose Stephen, a man full of faith and the Holy Spirit, and Philip, Prochorus, Nicanor, Timon, Parmenas, and Nicolas, a proselyte from Antioch.

Whom they set before the apostles; and when they had prayed, they laid hands on them.

Then the word of God spread, and the number of the disciples multiplied greatly in Jerusalem, and a great many of the priests were obedient to the faith (Acts 6:5-7).

What is the result of all these things coming together? It inspires unity. "The saying pleased the whole multitude" (Acts 6:5). Unity prevailed in the family of faith. It is interesting that of all the seven men who are listed in Acts 6:5 as the original deacon body, only three of them are ever mentioned again. This illustrates the principle that most of God's work is carried on by unknown, unsung heroes who quietly and without self-promotion carry out their God-given duties off the stage and away from the spotlight. When you see a healthy church you'll know it is because there have been generations of deacons who have lived their lives, tithed their income, been faithful to their church, and were serious about their task, and left a legacy for those who came after them. The integration of the deacon and the pastor inspires unity.

It also inspires the spreading of the Gospel. "Then the word of God spread and the number of the disciples multiplied greatly in Jerusalem" (Acts 6:7). Previously in Acts we hear how believers had been "added" to the church in Jerusalem. Now we read that the disciples "multiplied greatly" in Jerusalem. This always follows unity. Unity is the number one factor in church growth.

The ministry of the deacon finds its instigation in Acts 6. Every deacon should ask himself a question…"Why am I a deacon?" The very office of the deacon was born out of a problem. The deacon's primary task is to serve and to keep the unity in the church. It is not to dictate nor rule over the church. Initiation into this ministry is vitally important. What should characterize the deacon? He should be a true believer of good reputation, full of the Holy Spirit and full of wisdom. Next, integration is vital. How should the church be run? It should function by an integration of the ministry of the pastor and the deacon. The early church was wise in that it gave up leadership to the Apostles and they gave up ministry to the laymen. Finally, there's an inspiration in the functioning of the deacon ministry. It should all be about the business of inspiring unity which in turn inspires the ministry of the word which in turn inspires a multiplying of men and women coming to faith in Jesus Christ.

Our prayers should be that it might be said of the 21st century church of the Western world what was said of the 1st century church in Jerusalem, that "the word of God spread and the number of disciples multiplied greatly" (Acts 6:7).

Race Relations Day:
Discrimination

James 2.1-13

During the last few years of the 20th century some major changes have swept across our world. In the former Soviet Union, Jews who have been discriminated against for scores of years are being freed in growing numbers for emigration to Israel. The Berlin wall has crumbled. Eastern Europe is teaching us that no one can be suppressed and discriminated against indefinitely. In South Africa, change continues to be in the wind; the day is fast approaching when racial equality will exist in that strife-filled land. (Does that sound strange? We in America must remember that we are only one generation removed from racial segregation.)

Yet, in the Middle East discrimination is at an all-time high as Arab and Jewish conflict intensifies with each passing year. And in the United States there is still much racial discrimination between black and white, Jew and Gentile.

As the church lives in the third millennium, it must not avoid the issue of discrimination from without, or discrimination within. One would think after two thousand years of church history that James 2:1-13 would be irrelevant. Unfortunately, these verses are still extremely poignant.

The church of the Lord Jesus ought to be one place where discrimination is a dirty word. But not so! I am amazed at how few sermons can be found on the subject of discrimination in the church. Have you noticed how in some churches the congregation looks like they were all made from the same cookie cutter? They all look the same, dress the same, talk the same, and have the same hairstyle. They come from the same economic and social levels.

There are all kinds of subtle discrimination within the church. There is discrimination on the basis of race. Some people discriminate against blacks, whites, or Hispanics. Others discriminate on the basis of resources and have nothing to do with anyone who is not on their economic level. Some have no respect for others unless they are of the same social class or of the same sex.

Discrimination can work both ways. Christians with money discriminate against those without it. Christians without money discriminate against those who have money and respond with jealousy, envy, and suspicion. I know whites who discriminate against blacks and 1 know blacks who discriminate against whites. The same is true with Jews and Gentiles.

One of my fondest childhood memories was a trip to the circus at the old Will Rogers Coliseum in Fort Worth, Texas. I was particularly intrigued by a certain clown act. One of the clowns stood about eight feet tall. He was really not that tall. The truth is he was walking around on stilts and had long pants covering them. His partner was about three feet tall. These two clowns carried on in such a fashion that the whole audience was soon laughing uproariously. The tall man got the best of the short man until the final part of their act. Then the little person sneaked up behind the tall man and knocked the stilts out from under him, and he became a little person also. I tell that story to make a point. Discrimination — a cursed, dirty sin — stands on two stilts, two false legs that need to be knocked out from under it. One false leg is prejudice and the other is presumption. The intent of this message is to knock these false legs out from under this enemy of the cross.

The false leg of prejudice

 My brethren, do not hold the faith of our Lord Jesus Christ, the Lord of glory, with partiality.

For if there should come into your assembly a man with gold rings, in fine apparel, and there should also come in a poor man in filthy clothes,

And you pay attention to the one wearing the fine clothes and say to him, "You sit here in a good place," and say to the poor man, "You stand there,," or, "Sit here at my footstool,"

Have you not shown partiality among yourselves, and become judges with evil thoughts?

Listen, my beloved brethren: Has God not chosen the poor of this world to be rich in faith and heirs of the kingdom which He promised to those who love Him?

But you have dishonored the poor man. Do not the rich oppress you and drag you into the courts?

Do they not blaspheme that noble name by which you are called? (James 2:1-7).

An explanation

What is prejudice? It is defined as "bias because of a fixed idea; an opinion arrived at without taking time and care to judge fairly." Mark Twain said, "Prejudice is the ink with which all history is written." Many wars and major world conflicts have been the direct result of prejudicial thinking. Prejudice is one of the stilts on which discrimination stands.

James was firmly opposed to prejudice. He said, "Don't show favoritism" (James 2:1). The Greek word for "favoritism," prosopolepsia, literally means "to lay hold of one's face" — that is, to judge by how one appears to be on the outside. For example, when someone wears a certain type of jewelry or clothes, It is easy to make a judgment based on what we see on the outside. But James was saying, "Don't do this. Do not show favoritism. Do not just look at the outward appearance."

Prejudice can work both ways. While some people show favoritism to the rich and forget the outcasts, others show favoritism to the outcasts to the exclusion and disdain of the rich. Some are partial to the "haves" while others are partial to the "have-nots."

Prejudice is not just prevalent in politics, business, and social circles. It has found its way into many churches too. James' warning is particularly pertinent for churches. Remember, the Lord Jesus did not look on the outward appearance; He looked on the heart. He was not impressed by how many possessions people had, whom they knew, how high they had climbed up the social ladder, or how many times their pictures had appeared on the society page. He had as much respect for the poor widow as He did for wealthy Joseph of Arimathaea. Jesus was known for His compassion, not for compromise.

The people whom James addressed in his letter were flattering the rich in hopes of getting something from them. One wise old sage explained the difference between gossip and flattery: gossip is what we say behind someone's back that we would never say to his face; flattery is what we say to someone's face that we would never say behind his back. When a flatterer sees someone he hasn't seen in quite awhile, he says to her face, "Oh, you look so young." After she leaves he turns to a friend and says, "Isn't she looking old?"

James was saying, "Stop it! Do not show favoritism." We are to be like the Lord Jesus who looked on the heart. We are to love the rich and the outcasts alike. Whenever the church meets, everyone should be equal. No person in any fellowship is one bit better than my of the others. Prejudice in the Christian faith has no leg upon which to stand.

An illustration

James 2:2-4 illustrates this truth: "For if there should come into your assembly a man with gold rings, in fine apparel, and there should also come in a poor man in filthy clothes, and you pay attention to the one wearing the fine clothes and say to him, "You sit here in a good place," and say to the poor man, "You stand there," or, "Sit here at my foot-stool," have you not shown partiality among yourselves, and become judges with evil thoughts?"

Do you get the picture? A worship service is about to start. In walk two men. One is wearing a two-thousand-dollar designer suit, a gold watch, and a gold ring; the other comes in wearing clothes from the clothing ministry room. A certain usher, enamored with outward appearance, escorts the rich man to the best seat and says to the poor man, "Go stand over there, out of the way." The real problem here is not in finding a seat for the rich man, but in ignoring the poor man. We must remember the words of 1 Samuel 16:7: "The Lord does not see as man sees, for man looks at the outward appearance, but the Lord looks at the heart."

At this point many people try to make the Scriptures say something they are not saying. There's nothing wrong with wearing a gold ring or a gold watch. James was dealing with an issue far deeper than that. Gold rings were marks of social status in the first century. The man in James' story was wearing what he was wearing in order to draw attention to himself. It was his way of trying to be recognized and given a prominent seat. He was like the scribes and Pharisees whom our Lord rebuked: "They love the best places at feasts, the best seats in the synagogues" (Matt. 23:6).

Recently two men died whom God used to touch my life in special ways. One was a wealthy man by the world's stan-dards, probably a millionaire. For a generation he had been one of the backbones of our church. He sat about halfway back in the auditorium and never missed a service. He never pushed himself into leadership, but did more to help our church and people than any other man I have ever known. Time and again when I heard of a family struggling, I would call him and he would anonymously give money for rent or other emergencies. He used his contacts to help untold numbers of people find jobs. He was the greatest friend I have ever had, and I miss him very much.

The other man lived in an institutional retirement center not far from downtown Fort Lauderdale. His pants were about two sizes too big and the cuffs were rolled halfway up his calves so that his sockless feet and worn tennis shoes showed. His shirt was usually buttoned in the wrong holes, and there he would sit every Sunday morning on the front row. Only Heaven has recorded how many times I looked down into his face and breathed a prayer of thanksgiving to God for that man's presence. It constantly reminded me, as the preacher and pastor, of how welcome the outcasts of society should be in God's house.

We must be careful not to confuse the issue here. There is nothing wrong with wealth. "The love of money," not money, "is a root of all kinds of evil" (1 Tim. 6:10). Some people who have very little money love it more than those who are wealthy. It is not sinful to be rich, and it is not spiritual to be poor. There are many rich people who are spiritual, and many poor people who are sinful.

Another subtle danger in many churches, especially in times of financial crisis, is to cater to people who can help the church rather than cater to people the church can help. We ought always to fight this attitude. God has a way of taking care of everything else when we have our priorities in order.

Discrimination has no place in the church of the Lord Jesus. It stands on a shaky leg of prejudice, and James accused his readers of being guilty of this sin.

An accusation

James began his accusation by saying, "Listen, my beloved brethren" (James 2:5). He was teaching us the important lesson that when we confront our Christian brothers and sisters with their sins we should always do so in love. Before he made the accusation he wanted his brothers in Christ to know he loved them and was confronting them for their good and for God's glory.

The accusation is stinging: "You have dishonored the poor man" (James 2:6). The word for "insult," atimazo, is an aorist active verb that means "to treat without honor, to dishonor" — to take away one's dignity. If a poor man enters the house of God and receives discrimination instead of respect as a human being or a child of God, the last precious thing he possesses has been taken from him: his dignity and honor. We must guard against insulting anyone. Because Jesus said, "Whatever you did for one of the least of these brothers of mine, you did for me" (Matt. 25:40). James was saying, "Don't deny their dignity; don't steal their honor."

James 2:5 asks, "Has not God chosen the poor of this world to be rich in faith and heirs of the kingdom which He promised those who love Him?" Don't make the mistake of thinking that poverty makes a person one of God's favorites. That idea leads to a perverted kind of pride among the poor. The Greek word for "poor," ptochos, means "to crouch or cower with fear." James had in mind the kind of man who is humble in the presence of others and particularly in the presence of God. Those of us who have humbled ourselves and by faith trusted in the finished work of Christ on the cross are the ones who inherit the kingdom. The word for "inherit," kleronomos, means "to possess or to get ahold of." Those who love Christ have gotten hold of and possessed their inheritance.

Why is it that the poor seem to grasp the gospel in greater numbers than the rich and powerful? Is it because Christianity is not a thinking man's religion? No. In general the poor are more aware of their powerlessness and it is easier for them to acknowledge their need of salvation. Often the rich and powerful see no need of Christ. The greatest barrier to reaching them with the gospel is their pride and boasting, while the greatest barrier to reaching the poor with the gospel is sometimes their self-pity and bitterness.

James 2:6 says that the rich "exploit" (katadunasteuo) others. In Greek the word literally means "pressed down or to rule or to have power over." This strong word is used only one other time in all of Scripture. It is found in Acts 10:38 where reference is made to those who were "under the power of the devil." James was saying that we should all wake up and realize that the rich people we may be catering to are the very people who will exercise their power to bear down on us. He was saying that some rich people are ruthless oppressors.

James was accusing his readers of giving rich people

places of honor while pushing back into the corner the very people among whom Jesus spent His entire earthly ministry. It is a strong accusation, not a simple insinuation.

Jesus developed special relationships with the poor. He was born in the most impoverished circumstances imaginable. When He was dedicated in the temple His parents could only afford two turtle doves. In His first sermon He read from Isaiah: "The Spirit of the Lord is upon me, because He has anointed Me to preach the gospel to the poor" (Luke 4:18).

The more we become like Jesus, the more we will show mercy to the poor and rejected people of society, and the less we will "insult the poor." Jesus loves needy people. If only one institution in the world goes door to door seeking a bunch of poverty-stricken people who the world says will be liabilities instead of assets, it ought to be the New Testament church.

When our Lord went to Jerusalem He did not show favoritism. He talked to an invalid at the pool of Bethesda, and He also talked to Nicodemus, a ruler of the Jews. When Jesus went through Jericho He did not show favoritism. He called to rich Zacchaeus who was hiding in the tree, and He healed blind Bartimaeus who was begging by the roadside. Some churches today ignore the outcasts while other churches ignore the rich. But James said, "Do not show favoritism."

I love the sign that D. L. Moody placed over the door of his church in Chicago: "Ever welcome to this house of God are the strangers and the poor." Does this mean we should ignore the upper classes? No, we are to preach the gospel to every person. But we are never to neglect anyone, regardless of race, resources, or respectability. Quite frankly, if there is a segment of western society that the church has neglected, it is not the poor, but the rich. Jesus loved them all, just the same.

One reason the early church grew so rapidly was that prejudice was laid aside. Although the Jews and Samaritans hated each other, there was a place for Nicodemus, a ruler of the Jews, and a place for the woman of Samaria, who was formerly the town prostitute. In that early church there was a place for Onesimus, the former slave, and one for Philemon, his former master. Wealthy Barnabas gave a large parcel of real estate to the missionary church at Antioch, and alongside him was a place for a blind beggar who rattled a tin cup on the side streets of Jericho. The gospel gives everyone a place of dignity.

The vile sin of discrimination stands on two false legs that must be knocked from under it. One of those, as we've seen, is prejudice. The other is presumption.

The false leg of presumption

 If you really fulfill the royal law according to the Scripture, "You shall love your neighbor as yourself," you do well;

But if you show partiality, you commit sin, and are convicted by the law as transgressors.

For whoever shall keep the whole law, and yet stumble in one point, he is guilty of all.

For He who said, "Do not commit adultery," also said, "Do not murder." Now if you do not commit adultery, but you do murder, you have become a transgressor of the law.

So speak and so do as those who will be judged by the law of liberty.

For judgment is without mercy to the one who has shown no mercy. Mercy triumphs over judgment (James 2:8-13).

Those who discriminate are presumptuous. They presume upon three things: that discrimination is not sin, is not significant, and is not serious.

Presumption number one: Discrimination is not sin

Some people believe that discrimination is simply a way of life. How many times have we heard, "Well, I'm from the state of _____ and that's just the way things are over there." They falsely presume that God is just smiling and saying, "Oh yes, I know how it is." But in God's eyes that excuse is not cute; it is ugly. Discrimination is sin. To presume otherwise is to make a false presumption.

James 2:9 says, "If you show partiality, you commit sin and are convicted by the law as lawbreakers." The Greek word for "lawbreaker," *parabatai*, refers to a man who has a prescribed course to walk, but steps over the line and walks beside the intended path instead of on it; he deviates from God's intended course. When we discriminate and presume that we are not sinning, we step over the line as far as God is concerned. The Bible calls discrimination sin. God is as serious about the sin of prejudice as He is about the sin of perversion.

What should we do when we commit the sin of discrimination? Some say we should start trying to like or love the one against whom we discriminated. No! We should deal with discrimination as we would any other sin. We confess it to God and then forsake it.

James said that we are to abide by what he called the "royal law," which is to "love your neighbor as yourself" (James 2:8). The Lord Jesus said, "'You shall love the Lord your God with all your heart, with all your soul, and with all your mind.' This is the first and great commandment. And the second is like it: 'You shall love your neighbor as yourself.' On these two commandments hang all the Law and the Prophets" (Matt.22:37-40). Jesus put the first four commandments of the Decalogue into His first commandment, and the final six commandments of the Decalogue that have to do with our horizontal relationships in life — the royal law — into His second commandment. The royal law is not only given by the King of Kings, but it is also the king of all laws. It is the law of love that governs those who are citizens of Christ's kingdom.

Since as Christians we are under this royal law of love, what exactly is our relationship to the law? The legalists say we are bound to it and therefore should meet on the sabbath (which is Saturday). They say salvation is not obtained by grace and faith but by following the law. On the opposite end of the spectrum are the libertarians, who say that they are totally free from the law. They cite Romans 6:14 as their flagship verse: "For sin shall not have dominion over you, for you are not under law, but under grace." They lapse into what theologians call "antinomianism" ("against the law"). They think they are above the law.

Paul explained what the relationship of the Christian to the law should be: "What purpose then does the law serve? It was added because of transgressions, till the Seed should come to whom the promise was made; and it was appointed through angels by the hand of a mediator. But before faith came, we were kept under guard by the law, kept for the faith which would afterward be revealed. Therefore the law was our tutor to bring us to Christ, that we might be justified by faith. But after faith has come, we are no longer under a tutor" (Gal. 3:19,23-25).

The law was never given to save us. It was given to be our "schoolmaster" (KJV, *paidagogos*). The NIV translates this Greek word as "put in charge." *Paidagogos* could have been used in reference to a slave whose duty it was to see that a child made it to school safely and returned home at the end of the day. The law showed God's people how futile it was to think that they could get to Heaven by their own works — by keeping all the law. Thus, the law supervised their spiritual growth until the Messiah came. The law was the schoolmaster whose task was to bring people to Christ.

Does this mean that since Jesus has come we do not have to obey the law today? It means that Christians are under the royal law of love. Jesus did not do away with the law for Christians. In fact He said, "Do not think that I came to destroy the Law or the Prophets. I did not come to destroy but to fulfill. For assuredly, I say to you, till heaven and earth pass away, one jot or one tittle will by no means pass from the law till all is fulfilled" (Matt. 5:17-18). Jesus made the law a matter of the heart. He made it a matter of love. This was the original intention of God — the lawgiver — in the first place.

Paul wrote: "Stand fast therefore in the liberty by which Christ has made us free, and do not be entangled again with a yoke of bondage" (Gal. 5:1). The Christian is not governed by external laws and rules, but by the internal royal law — the law of love. When he loves God with all his heart, and loves his neighbor as himself, he will certainly live within the parameters of the moral code of the Mosaic law.

According to the royal law, discrimination really is sin. If a person discriminates against others, he does not have a leg on which to stand.

Presumption number two: Discrimination is not significant

Often people who discriminate are so blinded by what they feel that they think their sin is not significant. They reason, "So what...it's not like I murdered somebody or committed adultery; it's insignificant." What a presumption! James said that discrimination is significant. In fact he said that a person who discriminates is a lawbreaker like an adulterer or murderer.

James was writing to people who had the erroneous idea that petty sins of disrespect, favoritism, and discrimination are not significant. But James made clear what God really thinks about all types of sin.

Some people in our day seek to classify sin into different

categories. Up at the top is murder, followed by adultery, and then perhaps by stealing, etc. Down on the bottom of the list is discrimination. But God is revealing to us that one sin, no matter how insignificant we may think it to be, is significant: "For whoever shall keep the whole law, and yet stumble in one point, he is guilty of all. For He who said, 'Do not commit adultery,' also said, 'Do not murder.' Now if you do not commit adultery, but you do murder, you have become a transgressor of the law" (James 2:10-11). Without the mercy of God and the grace of the Lord Jesus Christ, one sin — no matter how small — is enough to condemn a person eternally. Jesus died for the sin of discrimination as much as for any other sin.

Many self-righteous people presume that because they have lived lives free of what society considers significant sins (murder, rape, and the like), God will just smile and pass over the sin of discrimination. If any of us share this presumption, we should look again at James 2:10.

James said if we "stumble" over just one law, it is as though we have broken all the laws. The Greek word translated "stumble," ptaio, means "to trip." Ptaio suggests a picture of a long road that is paved but has some rough spots over which the traveler stumbles. It doesn't matter that most of the road is paved if there is still a little patch that causes him to trip along the way. Ptaio also occurs in 2 Pet. 1:10: "Therefore, my brethren, be even more diligent to make your call and election sure, for if you do these things, you will never stumble." The point is, one little sin is like a rough place in the road. Even though all the rest of life's road is smooth, that one place can cause one to fall on his face.

D. L. Moody compared God's law to a ten-link chain onto which a man was holding while suspended over a great cliff. Moody said if all ten links were to break, the man would fall to his death. But if only one link were to break, the man would fall just as far and just as fast.

James 2:10 should put to rest the idea that any of us can get to Heaven on the basis of good works, reputation, or morality. We have all sinned and fallen short of the glory of God (Rom. 3:23) and thus we are all guilty of breaking all the law. We all need the redemptive work of Jesus. Perhaps Paul said it best: "For as many as are of the works of the law are under the curse; for it is written, 'Cursed is everyone who does not continue in all things which are written in the book of the law, to do them.' But that no one is justified by the law in the sight of God is evident, for 'the just shall live by faith.' Yet the law is not of faith, but 'the man who does them shall live by them.' Christ has redeemed us from the curse of the law, having become a curse for us (for it is written, 'Cursed is everyone who hangs on a tree'), that the blessing of Abraham might come upon the Gentiles in Christ Jesus, that we might receive the promise of the Spirit through faith" (Gal. 3:10-14).

It is strange how some people think that they can stand before the Judge of the universe and appeal to Him on the basis of the sins which they have not committed. That reasoning will go about as far with God as it would with a municipal judge if a person tried to get out of a speeding ticket by saying, "Judge, it is true that I broke the law and was going sixty miles per hour in a twenty-mile-per-hour school zone. But look at it this way — I never robbed a bank."

To be a lawbreaker, one does not have to break all the laws — only one. But to be a law-abider, one must keep all the laws. One way to break the royal law of love is to discriminate. Discrimination is a sin and it is significant. We must not presume otherwise.

Presumption number three: Discrimination is not serious

Some people are presumptuous enough to think that although discrimination may be sin and may be significant, it is really not serious. James challenged anyone who thinks this way to wake up. In God's eyes discrimination is very serious.

James 2:12-13 says, "So speak and so do as those who will be judged by the law of liberty. For judgment is without mercy to the one who has shown no mercy. Mercy triumphs over judgment." Which judgment was James referring to in these verses? After all, several judgments are mentioned in Scripture.

There is the judgment of the believer's sin (John 5:24). The Bible tells us that the believer will not come into condemnation because his sins have already been judged on Calvary's cross. There is also the judgment seat of Christ (2 Cor. 5:9-10) when the believer's works will be judged. Then there is the judgment of the nations (Matt. 25:31-32). This is not the final judgment of the lost, but the judgment that will deal with how people have treated the elect of Israel — the ones whom Jesus calls "these brothers of mine" in Matthew 25:40. This judgment will determine who can enter into the kingdom age and will be based on the nations' treatment of Israel during the period of tribulation. Finally, there is the judgment of the great white throne (Rev. 20:11), when the lost will be judged.

James was referring to the Judgment seat of Christ. There our words will be judged: "But I say to you that for every idle word men may speak, they will give account of it in the day of judgment. For by your words you will be justified, and by your words you will be condemned" (Matt. 12:36-37). Our works will also be judged at the judgment seat of Christ: "According to the grace of God which was given to me, as a wise master builder I have laid the foundation, and another builds on it. But let each one take heed how he builds on it. ...each one's work will become clear; for the Day will declare it, because it will be revealed by fire; and the fire will test each one's work, of what sort it is. If anyone's work which he has built on it endures, he will receive a reward. If anyone's work is burned, he will suffer loss; but he himself will be saved, yet so as through fire" (1 Cor. 3:10,13-15).

Because of the judgment to come, it is presumptuous to say that discrimination is not serious. James 2:12 is a call to action here. It says that we are to "*speak* and *act* as those who are going to be judged." These two verbs are in the continuous tense, which means that we are to keep on speaking and keep on acting. We should respond to the call with our lips — in our speech. We should respond with our lives — through our actions.

How can we speak and act as we should? By obeying the royal law, the "law that brings freedom" (James 2:12). We are to love God with all our hearts and our neighbors as ourselves. If we obey the law of love, we will want to obey all of God's other laws.

This royal law brings freedom. On the surface, law and liberty seem to stand in opposition to one another. They appear to be enemies. After all, law restrains liberty, and liberty seems to imply being freed from the law. But James was saying that law and liberty come together in beautiful harmony. The way to be really free is to live within the boundaries of God's law. When we do, we are free indeed. When we are really disciples of Jesus, we know the truth and the truth sets us free (John 8:31-32).

Those who live outside the parameters of God's law, on the other hand, are not really free. They cover over one lie with another lie. They are trapped into covering over one sin with another sin until they become slaves to a lifestyle of sinning. Yes, sin is serious and will be judged.

Yet James 2:13 says, "Mercy triumphs over judgment." If we show mercy to others in our speech and actions, we will triumph at the end at the judgment seat of Christ. The Greek word translated "triumph," *katakauchomai*, literally means "to have no fear of." Merciful people have no fear of judgment. The one who shows mercy in this life is not afraid of that day when he will stand before the great Judge who knows the secrets of all men's hearts. Yes, mercy triumphs over judgment.

But remember, James was talking here about the judgment of believers' works, not the judgment of sin. We are not saved by being merciful. We are saved by receiving mercy from Christ, and when we have received His mercy, we will show mercy.

If we are unmerciful — if we are guilty of discrimination — what can we do? Many say, "It's in my background." Well, just because your father was an adulterer, you do not have to be. Just because your father may have been a murderer, you do not have to be. We must deal with discrimination by seeing it as it is. It is sin. Thus we must deal with it like any other sin. After we admit it, confess it, and forsake it, we will begin to speak and act like followers of Christ. The church today needs to speak against discrimination and act against it by reaching out to others in mercy.

Thank God that Jesus was no respecter of persons. He did not show favoritism. He reached out to society's richest and society's poorest with the same intensity. I am so thankful He did not discriminate against me because of my race, my resources, my respectability, or the religion of my birth. Paul said, "For you know the grace of our Lord Jesus Christ, that though He was rich, yet for your sakes He became poor, so that you through His poverty might become rich" (2 Cor. 8:9). He showed mercy toward us with His lips and with His life. He spoke the world's greatest words and backed them up by going to the cross.

At Calvary the ground is level for the rich and poor alike. As Sunday School children sing, "Red and yellow, black and white — they are precious in His sight." Remember, in the end "mercy triumphs over judgment."

May we as followers of the Lord Jesus Christ heed the resolution on racial reconciliation which our Southern Baptist Convention passed at our 150th anniversary meeting in Atlanta, Georgia in June of 1995 saying:

> *WHEREAS, Since its founding in 1845, the Southern Baptist Convention has been an effective instrument of God in missions, evangelism, and social ministry; and*
>
> *WHEREAS, The Scriptures teach that Eve is the*

mother of all living (Gen. 3:20), and that God shows no partiality, but in every nation whoever fears him and works righteousness is accepted by him (Acts 10:34-35), and that God has made from one blood every nation of men to dwell on the face of the earth (Acts 17:26); and

WHEREAS, Our relationship to African-Americans has been hindered from the beginning by the role that slavery played in the formation of the Southern Baptist Convention; and

WHEREAS, Many of our Southern Baptist forbears defended the right to own slaves, and either participated in, supported, or acquiesced in the particularly inhumane nature of American slavery; and

WHEREAS, In later years Southern Baptists failed, in many cases, to support, and in some cases opposed, legitimate initiatives to secure the civil rights of African-Americans; and

WHEREAS, Racism has led to discrimination, oppression, injustice, and violence, both in the Civil War and throughout the history of our nation; and

WHEREAS, Racism has divided the body of Christ and Southern Baptists in particular, and separated us from our African-American brothers and sisters; and

WHEREAS, Many of our congregations have intentionally and/or unintentionally excluded AFrican-Americans from worship, membership, and leadership; and

WHEREAS, Racism profoundly distorts our understanding of Christian morality, leading some Southern Baptists to believe that racial prejudice and discrimination are compatible with the Gospel; and

WHEREAS, Jesus performed the ministry of reconciliation to restore sinners to a right relationship with the Heavenly Father, and to establish right relations among all human beings, especially within the family of faith.

Therefore, be it RESOLVED, That we, the messengers to the Sesquicentennial meeting of the Southern Baptist Convention, assembled in Atlanta, Georgia, June 20-22, 1995, unwaveringly denounce racism, in all its forms, as deplorable sin; and

Be it further RESOLVED, That we affirm the Bibles teaching that every human life is sacred, and is of equal and immeasurable worth, made in Gods image, regardless of race or ethnicity (Gen. 1:27), and that, with respect to salvation through Christ, there is neither Jew nor Greek, there is neither salve nor free, there is neither male nor female, for (we) are all one in Christ Jesus (Gal. 3:28); and

Be it further RESOLVED, That we lament and repudiate historic acts of evil such as slavery from which we continue to reap a bitter harvest, and we recognize that the racism which yet plagues our culture today is inextricably tied to the past; and

Be it further RESOLVED, That we apologize to all African-Americans for condoning and/or perpetuating individual and systemic racism in our lifetime; and we genuinely repent of racism of which we have been guilty, whether consciously (Psalm 19:13) or unconsciously (Leviticus 4:27); and

Be it further RESOLVED, That we ask forgiveness from our African-American brothers and sisters, acknowledging that our own healing is at stake; and

Be it further RESOLVED, That we hereby commit ourselves to eradicate racism in all its forms from Southern Baptist life and ministry; and

Be it further RESOLVED, That we commit ourselves to be doers of the Word (James 1:22) by pursuing racial reconciliation in all our relationships, especially with our brothers and sisters in Christ (1 John 2:6), to the end that our light would so shine before others, that they may see (our) good works and glorify (our) Father in heaven (Matt. 5:16); and

Be it finally RESOLVED, That we pledge our commitment to the Great Commission task of making disciples of all people (Matt. 28:19), confessing that in the church God is calling together one people from every tribe and nation (Rev. 5:9), and proclaiming that the Gospel of our Lord Jesus Christ is the only certain and sufficient ground upon which redeemed persons will stand together in restored family union as joint-heirs with Christ (Rom. 8:17).

Stewardship Sunday: Robbery without a weapon

(Malachi 3:7-12)

As far-fetched as it may seem, our finances generally mark the position of our spiritual pilgrimage. We are no farther along in our walk with God than the point to which we have learned to trust him with the tithe. Someone has well said more could be learned about a person's commitment by looking at their checkbook than their prayer book. This one area could be the reason for many unresolved conflicts and unmet needs.

The tithe is the place where many Christians go astray. Some because they have never been taught the spiritual truths concerning stewardship. Others because they have not studied the Word of God to find these truths for themselves. But mostly, I suppose, because of willful rebellion against the Word of God. Many Christians profess to love the Bible and take it as their rule of faith and yet deliberately ignore the plain teaching of the Word of God regarding the tithe. Some say the tithe is not applicable for us in this disposition of grace. My pastoral predecessor in Dallas, Dr. W. A. Criswell, puts it in perspective. He says, "Four hundred years before the giving of the law, father Abraham paid tithes to Melchizedek, the priest of the Most High God. Tithing was the foundation of the support of the worship of Israel throughout the centuries of the dispensation of the law. In that era, our Lord Jesus Christ lived and moved and had His being. It was He who said we ought to tithe" (Matt. 23:23b). In this new dispensation in which we now live (which continues unto the consummation of the age), it is our Lord Jesus Christ who receives our tithes, even though our human hands take it up in the congregations of the churches. "Here mortal men receive tithes, but there He receives them, of whom it is witnessed that He lives" (Heb. 7:8). To tithe is God's everlasting bond of fellowship between His people on earth and His Son, our Savior in Heaven.

Now, please do not misunderstand. This little message is not designed to "get more money for the church or for God's work." It is designed to lead you into spiritual growth and blessing by being obedient to the Word of God. One of the common complaints about many preachers is that "They are always preaching about money." It is usually a telltale sign that those who are making these statements are generally the ones who are disobedient to God's Word regarding the tithe.

There is a lot of misunderstanding today concerning the tithe (one-tenth of our income belonging to God). In fact, one of the great injustices that many of us preachers have done to the church is to insist that God demands one-tenth of our income and one-seventh of our week. This implies that the other nine-tenths of our income and the other six days of the week are ours to do with as we please. The truth of the matter is that everything we have belongs to God. Not just the tenth…everything! We are nothing more than stewards passing through this world. For most of you reading this message, 50 years from now everything you own will be in someone else's name. Fifty years ago what you own today belonged to someone else…your land, your home, your assets. When you came into this world you came into it naked without a dime. And the obvious truth that follows is that you will leave this world the same way. We do not own a thing. We are merely stewards of God's resources. Consequently, the tithe is a great place to start in our stewardship with God…but it is a terrible stopping place.

As our text unfolds before us we will see the whole emphasis of the Word of God is not on our giving as much as it is on his opening the windows of heaven to pour us out a blessing that there would not be room enough to receive. God wants to bless us far more than we want a blessing. The tithe is a starting place in getting God into action in the affairs of man. Let's venture into the realm of this exciting journey with God that promises to "Open for you the windows of heaven and pour out for you a blessing until it overflows. We note first in our text:

God's apparent problem with us!

 "Yet from the days of your fathers you have gone away from My ordinances and have not kept them. Return to Me, and I will return to you," says the Lord of hosts.

But you said, "In what way shall we return?"

Will a man rob God? Yet you have robbed Me!
But you say, "In what way have we robbed You?"
In tithes and offerings.

You are cursed with a curse, for you have robbed
Me, even this whole nation (Mal. 3:7-9).

We have before us God's problem with us. We see initially that this problem is personal. "You have robbed me!" (Note the personal pronouns). Have you ever been the victim of robbery? I talked recently with one of our ladies in the church whose home had been broken into, all her cabinets ransacked, money stolen along with valuable papers, and many sentimental items of great value were also stolen including the wedding ring of her deceased husband. Her anguish was intensified by the fact that someone, uninvited, had invaded the privacy of her own domain and took items of value that belonged to her. You see, robbery is a very personal matter and only one who has been a victim of such an experience can know the real anguish of heart. God's apparent problem with us is personal. He said, "You have robbed me!" This is a strong accusation and not a mere insinuation. He calls to us in Malachi 3:7 saying, "Return to Me, and I will return unto you." The point of return is always the point of departure. And God said the place of departure for many of us was the matter of the tithe.

Here is God's apparent problem with us. It is robbery without a weapon. "You have robbed me!" But the truth is when we rob God there are some other things we rob in the process. When we do not faithfully bring the tithe to God we rob the church of its ministry. We also rob the world, through great missionary enterprises, of the gospel. But even more personally, we rob ourselves of great blessing. "It is more blessed to give than to receive."

In the New Testament we find these words escaping the lips of our Lord, "Render therefore unto Caesar the things that are Caesar's and unto God the things that are God's." Isn't it amazing that some church members would never entertain the thought of not paying their taxes (that is rendering unto Caesar the things that are Caesar's). Many of us would never think of not paying taxes on our home, sales taxes, or internal revenue taxes. And yet, many of us never render unto God the things that are God's! This is God's apparent problem with us. It is a personal problem. We have robbed him.

As the text unfolds we see that the problem is not only personal but it is also pointed. God says "You have robbed me." We answer back, "How have we robbed thee?" And his answer comes in a very pointed way, "In tithes and offerings." Tithing is God's appointed program for us. It always has been and it always will be. There are some today who say that the tithe is merely an Old Testament law and is not applicable for this dispensation of grace. The truth of the matter is the tithe existed among the people of God long before the law was given. In Genesis 14:20 we see Abraham giving the tithes to Melchizedek. In Genesis 28:19-22 we see Jacob vowing to give a tenth unto the Lord. When the law was given the tithe was definitely incorporated in it. "And all the tithe of the land, whether of the seed of the land, or of the fruit of the tree, is the Lord's: it is holy to the Lord" (Lev. 27:30). In the New

Testament we see Jesus approving and obviously practicing the tithe. The Pharisees were out to catch him at any point they could. Certainly had Jesus been failing on the matter of the tithe, he would have had stern fingers of accusation pointed in his way. Note what he says in his rebuke of the Pharisees in Matthew 23:23 "Woe to you, scribes and Pharisees, hypocrites! for you pay tithe of mint and anise and cumin, and have neglected the weightier matters of the law: justice and mercy and faith. These you ought to have done, without leaving the others undone." This verse is often misunderstood and misinterpreted. Here Jesus is rebuking the Pharisees for their hypocrisy, not for their tithing. In fact he says, "These things ought ye to do." The word "ought" is an imperative and is translated in other versions as "must". Jesus saw the tithe as a requirement from God. It is unthinkable in light of the cross on which our Savior died, that any of us under grace would give less than the Jews gave under law! It is helpful in our understanding of the tithe to know that it is holy unto the Lord. "And all the tithe of the land, whether of the seed of the land, or of the fruit of the tree, is the Lord's: it is holy unto the Lord" (Lev. 27:30). The Bible says that "the tithe is holy unto the Lord." That is to say, God reserves for himself, as his own, one tenth of what he gives to us. It is holy unto him. Now, there are not many things called holy in the Word of God. When something is set aside as holy it is a dangerous thing to keep that from the Lord. You may say, "But I can't afford to tithe." The very reason you think you can't is no doubt because you have robbed God of something that is holy to him. Note also that the text says, "the tithe is the Lord's!" This ought to open our eyes to a misconception that has blinded many from the truth of the Scripture. That is that one-tenth of our income is not our own personal property at all. It does not belong to us. We have no say-so about it whatsoever. "The tithe is the Lord's!" I didn't say it…God said it! Regardless of what we have done with it. It is the Lord's. God's tithe may be on your back in the form of a new suit of clothes. It may be at your home in the form of a new video game for your television set. You may be watching the Lord's tithe each evening on a new color television set in your den. You may be driving the Lord's tithe down the street in the form of a new car. You may be investing the Lord's tithe in a bank or another investment institution. You may be stealing it, robbing it, driving it, wearing it, investing it, but it is still not yours…the tithe is the Lord's!

Yes, we need to change our mentality that we give the tithe. No, the tithe is the Lord's. God says to withhold the tithe is the same as robbing his own treasury. The tithe belongs to God and in reality we do not give anything to Him until we give over the tithe.

It is indeed a penetrating question, "Will a man rob God?" Friend, I would rather rob The First National Bank than to rob God. It doesn't matter who we are or what we have, we need to tithe. The worse our financial condition the more we need to tithe. The tithe is holy. It is the Lord's. There is a blessing when we give it and a curse when we steal it according to the Bible. The Bible warns us plainly, do not touch the tithe. We tithe because we love the Lord Jesus Christ. A Christian should tithe for the same reason he keeps all the other commandments. If we render unto Caesar the things that are Caesar's, let us also render unto God the things that are God's. Here is God's apparent problem with us, it is personal and it is pointed. Let us note secondly:

God's appointed program for us!

 "Bring all the tithes into the storehouse, that there may be food in My house, and try Me now in this," says the Lord of hosts, "If I will not open for you the windows of heaven and pour out for you such blessing that there will not be room enough to receive it" (Mal. 3:10).

If we are indeed guilty of robbing God of the tithe, then certainly there must be some program of rehabilitation to bring us into right relationship with him. God lays down this appointed program for us in text above. Note first the plan. "*Bring* all the tithes into the storehouse." Every word of Scripture is important. Note that God told us to bring the tithes, not send them. The Wise Men did not send their gifts of gold, frankincense, and myrrh to the Christ child, they brought them! The woman with the alabaster box did not send the box for Jesus' anointing, she brought it! God says that we are to bring the tithe. In the act of bringing there is personal worship. This is God's plan — "bring."

Secondly note the person. "Bring (Bring *ye*, KJV) all the tithes into the storehouse." You bring! You bring the tithe because you are commanded to bring it and love obeys. John Bisagno has well said in his book, *The Word of the Lord*, "All through the Scripture love is equated with action." Jesus asked, "Lovest thou me?...feed my sheep." At another time he asked, "Lovest thou me?...keep my commandments." He said, "He that heareth my words and doeth them, he it is who loveth me." Love is something we do. Love doesn't sing, "Oh how I love Jesus," love tithes! You can tithe without loving. But you cannot love without tithing!

I am always a little intrigued by bumper sticker evangelism. We have all seen the bumper stickers that declare, "Honk if you love Jesus." However, the latest ones contain a lot more truth. They say, "Tithe if you love Jesus — anybody can honk!"

Thirdly, note the proportion in God's appointed program for us. "Bring all the *tithes* into the storehouse." I Corinthians 16:1-2 says: "Now concerning the collection for the saints, as I have given orders to the churches of Galatia, so you must do also: On the first day of the week let each one of you lay something aside, storing up as he may prosper, that there be no collections when I come." Note those words, "as he may prosper." This signifies a definite proportion of income..."as he may prosper." It does not say let each one of you lay something aside "as he feels led!" Nor does it say let each one of you lay something aside "as he feels moved by the Holy Spirit." Friend, the Holy Spirit will never lead us to do anything contrary to the Word of God. And the Word of God teaches us that the tenth is the Lord's. The Bible says let each one of you lay something aside "storing up as he may prosper." That is, in a proportionate way, according to a percentage basis. This makes giving equal. The millionaire and less wealthy person are equal in their giving in relationship "as he may prosper." Thus we see that the proportion of our giving is the tithe.

Next the text reveals to us the *place* of our tithes. "Bring all the tithes into the storehouse." Where is the storehouse? Again, I

Corinthians 16:1-2 says we are to "lay in store." This clearly points us back to Malachi 3:10 which says for us to "Bring all the tithes into the___?" To the what? To the storehouse! Also note when we are to do this. "On the first day of the week." Now, what happens on the first day of the week? Obviously, the local New Testament church is at worship. And the truth of the Scripture is that the local church is the storehouse! In the New Testament over 90 percent of the time the word "church" is mentioned it refers to that local, first day worshipping, body of baptized believers. It is not our privilege to scatter our tithe around to all sorts of parachurch organizations, evangelism organizations, youth groups, etc. They are to receive offerings, not tithes! The tithe is to be brought to the storehouse on the first day of the week. That is, the local New Testament church. And by the way, don't sell the church short. It will still be here when all the other organizations and groups are dead and gone. Any organization that does not originate in, cooperate with, and build up the local New Testament church will come to naught. The place of the tithe is the storehouse, the church.

The text also reveals to us the purpose. "Bring all the tithes into the storehouse that there may be food in My house." The purpose of bringing the tithe is to further the work of Christ through the church in bringing salvation to men and women. This is our good and godly purpose given to us by the Lord Jesus Christ in the great commission.

Finally, note the *proposition*. "Bring all the tithes into the storehouse that there may be food in My house, and try Me now in this." This is unbelievable! God is saying to you, "Put me (Almighty God) on trial. Prove me, try me, with the tithe!" Here is the only directive in the Scripture that can be put on a trial basis. "Try me, prove me," God says. We are challenged to return to Him the one-tenth that is rightfully His and see whether He will let us be the loser or not. This is amazing condescension that God allows Himself to be put on trial by us in such a manner. If there is any doubt as to God's existence here is the way to prove Him. What a proposition — try me, prove me, put me to the test!

God's appointed program for us is definitely the tithe. The tithe is a great place to start but a miserable place to stop in our stewardship. In fact, in the purest Biblical sense, a tither is simply a reformed thief.

What happens when we become aware of God's apparent problem with us, and meet the conditions of God's appointed program for us? Note finally:

God's abundant promise to us!

 "Bring all the tithes into the storehouse, that there be food in My house, and try Me now in this," says the Lord of hosts, "If I will not open for you the windows of heaven and pour out for you such blessing that there will not be room enough to receive it."

"And I will rebuke the devourer for your sakes, so that he will not destroy the fruit of your ground, nor shall the vine fail to bear fruit for you in the field," says the Lord of hosts.

"And all nations will call you blessed, for you will be a delightful land," says the Lord of hosts (Mal. 3:10-12).

Oh, the promises of God that are ours for the claiming! We see first that there is the promise of provision. God says to us that he "will open the windows of heaven and pour us out a blessing that there will not be room enough to receive." There has never been a time when we more needed to know how to open the windows of heaven than today. Remember, these promises are contingent upon our returning to God in the matter of the tithe.

Note that this promise of provision involves quality. These blessings come right out of heaven. They are supernatural. God says, "I will open the windows of heaven, and pour you out a blessing." He will "pour out." They will be sudden. Have you ever poured tea from a pitcher? If you are not careful it will pour out in rapid force. God says our promise of provision will be right out of heaven. What does it mean that He will "open the windows of heaven?" Let's let Scripture interpret Scripture. Listen to Genesis 7:11-12: "In the six hundredth year of Noah's life, in the second month, the seventeenth day of the month, the same day were all the fountains of the great deep broken up, and the windows of heaven were opened. And the rain was upon the earth forty days and forty nights." Here the identical expression is used. This same expression used with the deluge of the flood is the same expression used in Malachi 3 in God's response to our tithe. God has promised to honor us with an abundant out-pouring! And we are not talking about only spiritual blessings but temporal blessings. The truth of the Scriptures is that we "reap what we sow." If we sow oats we will reap oats. If we sow wheat we will reap wheat. The laws of the harvest simply stated are that we always reap what we sow, we always reap after we sow, and we always reap more than we sow. Surely we do not suppose the lover of our soul will allow us to be the loser because we are faithful to His Word and obedient to His will. I have never seen nor heard of a consistent tither who did not find this to be true. The reason so many are in financial straits today is the simple fact that they have robbed God.

The promise of provision not only involves quality but involves quantity. Notice the quantity of the blessing, "there shall not be room enough to receive it." This simply means we shall have to give it away. This more than enough blessing is for all who meet His conditions. Isn't this a far cry from the haunting need today where so many are crying "not enough!" Man's rebellion leads to this kind of economy...the cry of "not enough!" But not God's. His abundant promise to us is that He will open the windows of heaven and pour out a blessing for us we will not have room enough to receive. This is the John 6 principle in action. (The boy gave his lunch of a few fish sandwiches and thousands of people were fed and basketful were left over). John Bunyan is reported to have said, "There was a man; some called him mad; the more he gave; the more he had!" This is God's promise of provision in a nutshell involving quality along with quantity.

But there is also the promise of protection involved here. God says "I will rebuke the devourer for your sakes." Here is quite a promise! When we return to God with the tithe we step into the supernatural protection of God. I'll confess to you that I do not know all the ramifications of this promise. But that does not mean I do not choose to abide in them. It is a promise that God will supernaturally give protection. If the devourer is a plague on our crops, God says He will devour him, "I will rebuke him." If the devourer is recession, God says I will rebuke him in your behalf. God gives supernatural protection to the consistent tither. It is His abundant promise to us.

Now, we are commanded to tithe not because God is dependent upon our gifts of money. This brings the wrong concept of our sovereign God. He is certainly not dependent upon you nor me. The truth is, God doesn't need our money. He commands us to tithe in order that we might get involved in His program of economy that unlocks the floodgates of blessing upon us. The whole significance of this passage of Scripture is that when the tithe is presented it releases the vast treasures of heaven and moves God into action in our behalf. It always has and it always will!

God's apparent problem with us is obvious. It is personal, "You have robbed me." It is pointed, "in tithes." But God doesn't leave us in this sad condition for we see God's appointed program for us. The plan "bring," the person "you," the proportion "all the tithe," the place "into the storehouse," the purpose "that there may be food in My house," and the proposition "and try Me now in this." Almighty God is saying to us, "Put me on trial. Try Me now in this." And once we have met this program we see God's abundant promise to us. The promise of provision and the promise of protection. "If you return to me...I'll return to you." Here is God's promise to you today.

The tithe is the Lord's. It is holy unto Him. And He led the way...The greatest stewardship verse in the Word of God is found in John 3:16, "For God so loved the world that He gave His only begotten son that whosoever believeth in him shall not perish but have everlasting life." In light of this cross upon which our Saviour died the question of our text has penetrating proportions..."Will a man rob God?"

Some practical suggestions

Many say, "I know I need to be obedient to God with the tithe but I just can't seem to get started." The following are a few simple and proven practical suggestions:

(1) Make it a matter of definite prayer.

(2) The Bible speaks of our giving of "the first fruits." Each time you deposit your paycheck make sure the first check you write is "unto the Lord." Give the tithe priority over everything else. Remember, the tithe is the Lord's."

(3) Be just as strict and systematic with the tithe as you are in business matters. In fact, even more so, for it belongs to God.

(4) Always rest in the fact we can trust the Lord. There has never been a consistent tither who was sorry he tithed. The Lord Jesus, who gave Himself for you, will not allow you to be the loser because you are faithful to His Word and obedient to His will.

(5) Go ahead...and do it! "Try Me," says the Lord, "If I will not open the windows of heaven and pour you out a blessing that there will not be room enough to receive." "Return to me...and I will return to you."

Thanksgiving Day:
Where are the nine?

Luke 17:11-19

Thanksgiving is one of America's favorite holidays. Unfortunately, in our modern culture it has come to be more identified with the Macy's Day Parade or Dallas Cowboy football or turkey dinners. It seems fewer and fewer Americans set aside the day to give thanks to God for His blessings upon us.

Thanksgiving Day meant something far different to our forefathers. Our history reveals that our nation was settled by those who were followers of the Lord Jesus Christ. Don't believe the revisionists who are rewriting our American History books. Ours is a Christian heritage. The first permanent settlement in America was at Plymouth. It was settled by the Pilgrims who were a group of Christian separatists that broke with the Church of England. On September 16, 1620 they sailed from Plymouth, England to America on the Mayflower. Before they landed they penned and signed what has come to be known as the Mayflower Compact. While still on board the ship they set forth the fact that

213

they wanted to establish a colony that was based on biblical principles. Their signatures acknowledged God's sovereignty in their lives and their need to obey Him. They signed a document that declared they were establishing a new colony in the New World "for the glory of God and the advancement of the Christian faith." Out of the 103 who landed, 51 died the first winter. After the harvest of that first year, Governor William Bradford proclaimed a day of thanksgiving and prayer. The custom prevailed until Abraham Lincoln made it an official American holiday during the days of the Civil War.

Much of the secularization of America has done away with the original meaning of Thanksgiving. No longer do most Americans see their existence on this soil "for the glory of God and the advancement of the Christian faith." If anyone on earth should be giving thanks to God it is those of us who are living in the United States of America.

Someone has noted that if you reduce the world population to 1,000 and put them all in one city it would have quite a distinctive look. Only 46 of that 1,000 would be Americans. Nine hundred and fifty-four would represent the rest of the world. Yet, these 46 would receive half of the income from the entire city. These 46 people's life expectancies would be 75 years of age while the rest would be 40 years of age. These 46 people would eat 70% above the daily food requirement while 80% of the rest of the city would never get a balanced meal. In fact, the kitchen disposals of the 46 people would eat better than 80% of the city.

We are a blessed people. However, I fear we're not a thankful people. Even within the American church, such things as pluralism, humanism, and secularism have seen to that. And yet, the giving of thanks is a powerful phenomenon with a liberating effect.

There is an encounter near the end of Christ's earthly life that has been recorded for all posterity which gives a formula for putting thanksgiving into our lives in such a way that it brings wholeness and purpose. We find our Lord en route to Jerusalem. As He passed through the regions of Samaria and Galilee, as He enters a certain village, He encountered 10 men who are lepers who lifted up their voices calling out for mercy. Jesus spoke healing to them and sent them to show themselves to the priests. Only one of them returned to give thanks to God. Jesus asked a penetrating question, "Where are the nine?" The response to these ten lepers is revealing. The Lord Jesus is showing us there are three actions we should take to live life to its fullest. We should get up. This has to do with fortitude. If we don't, we might miss the Master. We should get out. This has to do with attitude. If we don't, we might miss the miracle. Finally, we should get back. This has to do with gratitude. If we don't, we might miss the moment.

Get up. This has to do with fortitude. If we don't we may miss the Master.

 Now it happened as He went to Jerusalem that He passed through the midst of Samaria and Galilee. Then as He entered a certain village, there met Him ten men who were lepers, who stood afar off. And they lifted up their voices and said, "Jesus, Master, have mercy on us!" (Luke 17:11-13).

Do you get the picture? Jesus passes through a certain village and is met by 10 lepers. They had heard the reports, strange rumors, how He had touched lepers and made them pure. They "stood afar off" because they could not get close. Mosaic law isolated lepers from social contact. They were forbidden to come within six feet of a whole person. If the wind was blowing they couldn't come within 50 yards. If someone inadvertently approached them they were commanded to shout, "unclean, unclean."

So what did these lepers do when Jesus was passing by? They got up. This showed a great amount of fortitude. They began to shout, "Jesus, Master, have mercy on us." They could have sat there in their hopelessness but they didn't. Look at them. They're all alike. They're all lepers. They all suffer from the same hideous disease. It slowly eats away at the body erasing facial features first. Then the fingers; the hands are frozen into claws before they simply fall off. The feet are filled with sores and become bandaged stumps before they're left behind. The odor was nauseating. The appearance was ghastly. The leper had no competitor. He suffered the fate of a long, slow, agonizing death lived out in some leper colony isolated from friends and family. The leper was an outcast. He was shut off. A leper in the first century was always simply an abandoned bit of human wreckage living in hopelessness.

All of these 10 men had a desperate determination to live. Though the future seemed futile, these particular men refused to give up. When they hear that Jesus is passing by they all go out to see Him. They all appeal to Him for help. It is interesting that they did not appeal for justice. They appealed for mercy.

They did not ask Christ to bless them on the basis of what they deserved. They cried out for mercy.

Some of us live in constant defeat because we're holding out for justice. Perhaps someone has wronged us and we harbor resentment for years. We want justice. Some of us have been abused. We want justice. However, justice belongs to God. Give it over to Him. Truth will always win in the end. Our plea should be one for mercy.

The Lord Jesus was passing by and here were ten men who got up with fortitude and did not miss the Master. Is there anyone sitting beside this road this morning? Time and again Jesus has passed by but you never called out to Him. Or, maybe you sought comfort in those around you but found generally just misery. On Thanksgiving Day it is time to get up. This has to do with fortitude. If we don't we might miss the Master.

Get out. This has to do with attitude. If we don't we may miss the miracle.

 So when he saw them, He said to them, "Go, show yourselves to the priests." And so it was that as they went, they were cleansed (Luke 17:14).

Do you have a mental picture? Not only do these men get up but they got out. They obey the Lord which is evidence of the fact that they believe. What an attitude we see here. They were not healed at this particular point. They were still lepers. A leper was to show himself to the priest after he had been healed. It took faith for these men to act in obedience to God's word and go show themselves to the priests while they were still lepers. And thus the Bible says, "So it was as they went, they were cleansed!"

Jesus said, "Go show yourself to the priest." This immediately presented a bit of a problem for these 10 men. Only cleansed lepers were to do this according to Leviticus chapters 13 and 14. To hear this command is one thing but to get up and get out with nothing but faith in Christ's word is another thing. Implicit in this command was if they went, they would be healed. At this point they are still lepers. Thus, it all boils down to one simple fact. The only way to test the value of Christ's words is to obey them!

And so they take him at his word and get out. What an attitude of faith. They start to walk. Many of us know little of this journey to the priests. They got up and got out by faith at the word of Christ when they had not seen it yet. Many of us live here in these verses. We have the word from God but we've not seen it yet. But we're walking. We're not going to stop at simply getting up, we're going to get out. Too many lepers never start walking until they can see it. And thus they spend their days with hope lost and gone.

I like the way B. B. McKinney said it back in 1934.

> *Have faith in God when your pathway is lonely.*
> *He sees and knows all the ways you have trod.*
> *Never alone are the least of his children.*
> *Have faith in God, have faith in God.*
> *Have faith in God when your prayers are unanswered.*
> *Your earnest plea He will never forget.*
> *Wait on the Lord, trust His word and be patient.*
> *Have faith in God, He'll answer yet.*

Have faith in God though all else fail around you.
Have faith in God, He provides for His own.
He cannot fail though all kingdoms shall perish.
He rules, He reigns upon His throne.
Have faith in God He's on the throne.
He cannot fail, He must prevail,
have faith in God, have faith in God.

The Bible simply says, "As they went, they were cleansed." The language of the New Testament, the passive voice here, leaves no doubt that it was God who performed the miracle! All of them, on the way, as they went, were cleansed! Think about it. All they had was the word of Christ. All they had was the promise of God. They walked in faith and obedience.

Before every great miraculous work of God, He moves us out where all we have is His promise. This is the faith life. "As they went." Those words have never been spoken of some of us. Oh, we might get up and call for mercy, but too few of us get out and walk in obedience to God's word. Had they not done this they would have missed the miracle. Look at the 10 lepers. Now they are clean. All they had to hold to was the word of Christ. They did and He was true to that word. They got up and then they got out in faith. Faith is the victory!

Get back. This has to do with gratitude. If we don't we may miss the moment.

 And one of them, when he saw that he was healed, returned, and with a loud voice glorified God,

> *And fell down on his face at His feet, giving Him
> thanks. And he was a Samaritan.*
>
> *So Jesus answered and said, "Were there not ten
> cleansed? But where are the nine?*
>
> *Were there not any found who returned to give glory
> to God except this foreigner?"*
>
> *And He said to him, "Arise, go your way. Your faith
> has made you well." (Luke 17:15-19)*

Look at these 10 men. They were all lepers. They all called
on the Lord Jesus. They all stepped out in faith. They all were
healed. They all got up. They all got out. But here the likeness ends.

Stand with them there on that road for a moment. They look
at themselves and all of a sudden they realize they are clean.
They're amazed. They begin to hug one another. Then one of
them says, "I haven't held my wife in months." A moment later
we look and he's running down the road to toward his home.
Another says, "I have never seen my newborn son." And he too
is gone. Another quickly exclaims, "I haven't been to my shop
in almost a year." And he is off and running. One by one
they're all gone. But no. There is one left standing in the road
alone. The other nine are never heard from again. Oh, they got
up and they got out, but they never got back.

Look at the one solitary man who stands in the road. He
too is looking down the road toward his home. He too has a
family. He too has a business. He too has friends. But something is more pressing. He has to get back. This has to do with
gratitude. If he doesn't, he may miss the moment. Is there

anyone on that road today? Once you were in a crisis. Once you've gotten up and called for mercy. Once you too got out and walked in faith, but when the blessing came you forgot to get back with gratitude and in so doing you missed a moment, a very important moment.

Note the Bible says, "And one of them" (Luke 17:15). I'm sorry to say we do not know his name. He is simply referred to as "one of them." His name is never left for us. He belongs to that vast company of people who live their beautiful lives and do their worthwhile deeds without ever telling us who they are. We do not know his name but he is shouting to us today to "get back." It has to do with gratitude. If we don't we might miss the moment."

Look at him. He returned and "with a loud voice glorified God" (Luke 17:15). Why was he so demonstrative? I tried to put myself by his side on that road as I read this text. You know what I would have found myself doing? I think I might have been standing there alongside of him, putting my arm around his shoulder and trying to calm him. Some of us are not comfortable with loud doxologies and loud hallelujahs. Well, that is our loss, not His. For some of us it's been too long since we've felt the touch of the Master's hand.

Why is it that so many of us are like the 10 who call on the Lord Jesus when we're in times of need and so few of us know much about praise and thanksgiving? This man went back and "fell down on his face at His feet giving Him thanks. And he was a Samaritan" (Luke 17:16). Do you see any difference here? In verse 12 they "stood afar off." But now we find this man at Jesus' feet. That is what cleansing will do for you. The Bible says, "And he was a Samaritan." The "he" is emphatic. That is, HE was a Samaritan! Here was a man distant to the covenant promises. He was like the woman in Samaria and the man on the Jericho road. Here we see the missionary heart of our Lord.

Jesus then asks three rhetorical questions designed to cause us to be reflective upon this encounter. "Were not 10 cleansed?" Yes! "Where are the nine?" The question in Greek is emphatic and reads, "the nine ...*where*?" He was not asking for an answer. He was making an observation. They had missed the moment. Then he asks, "Were there not any found who returned to give glory to God except this foreigner?" I'm afraid too many of us in America find ourselves in the company of the nine. Once we got up and got out but then we went on our own way when the blessings came.

Why didn't they return? Did they feel they deserved this miracle? Human nature has a way of always claiming our own rights. I put myself on this road recently. When I see so many heartbroken kids without mothers to nurture them, I ask myself did I deserve to have a mother who sacrificed so much for me? When I see so many kids with dads who have no time, did I deserve to have had a dad who always encouraged me and never missed an event in which I participated? When I visit folks in the hospital who are sick and now know I've had over a half a century of excellent health, I sense the blessing of God. When I see parents whose kids have broken their hearts and my wife and I have had two daughters who brought us nothing but joy and honor, do I really deserve this? When I know men whose wives have been unfaithful, do I deserve the good and godly one that Christ has given me? When I hear pastor friends whose church has caused them consternation and heartache and pain, do I deserve to have pastored the wonderful churches I was blessed to serve over the pastoral ministry I received from Him? When I hear men and women who talk of having no real lifelong friends, do I deserve the faithful friends I've enjoyed over the decades? When I see the heartbreak today in Third World countries around the world, do I deserve to have been born in the state of Texas with all the privileges it affords? When I see men and women who live their lives in sin and shame with guilt and defeat written across their faces, do I deserve to have been forgiven by the grace of God? The answer is a simple one. I deserved none of this. It is all unmerited favor and grace, marvelous grace.

I hope Thanksgiving is more to all of us than simply parties and football games and parades. The Lord Jesus is still asking, "Where are the nine?" Are any of the nine reading this volume?

Then Jesus said to this one, "Arise, go your way. Your faith has made you well" (Luke 17:19). The important fact here is that the Lord of this universe wants to be thanked. Hebrews 13:15-16 says, "Therefore by Him let us continually offer the sacrifice of praise to God, that is, the fruit of our lips, giving thanks to His name. But do not forget to do good and to share, for with such sacrifices God is well pleased."

Grace works in surprising places. Only the Samaritan heard the Lord Jesus say, "Your faith has made you well." He became whole on the inside as well as the outside. The other nine hurried on to the priest to be declared clean. But this one was declared whole, well, by the Lord Jesus Christ himself!

Are we really that far removed from this scene? The disease of sin is far more dangerous than leprosy. One destroys the body but sin destroys the body and the soul. Desperation may bring you to Christ but only gratitude can keep you there. Where are the nine?

Thanksgiving Day. What will it be for you? Will you get up? Will you get out? The real question is, will you get back? May we begin to lead America back to our place at Christ's feet and renew the pledge of the Mayflower Compact that we're here, "for the glory of God and the advancement of the Christian faith." Jesus is passing by. Where are the nine?

World Missions Day:
Moving out of our comfort zones

Matthew 9:35-38

Comfort zones are areas from which we seldom stray. Some have social comfort zones and have little contact with anyone outside their own socioeconomic level. Others have political comfort zones and do not have much to do with those who do not share their political persuasion. Some of us even have our comfort zones in the church. We all have little comfort zones whether they be in literature or the arts or music or sports or whatever. It is easy to get comfortable and never venture out of a comfort zone. Comfort zones take the cutting edge out of many lives.

When we study the life of our Lord we find that He was continually moving men and women out of their comfort zones. He called those fishermen up in Galilee to throw down their nets and follow Him. That is, He called them to leave the comfort zone of their surroundings. Everywhere He went He called upon people to leave their comfort zones whether it was Zachias down in Jericho, or the rich young ruler, or the woman at the well in Samaria.

Comfort zones keep us from our potential. In the business world salesmen can gravitate toward them. We're even prone to find our comfort zones in our own ecclesiology. Comfort zones kill productivity and production.

The Lord Jesus came into this world. Now, if we want to think of leaving a comfort zone think of Him. He laid aside His glory and came to walk the dust of this earth. And with whom? Publicans and sinners and the despised and the multitudes. And then His followers impacted the world in one generation. How? They moved out of their comfort zones. On World Mission's Day this is a word to those of us who have gotten comfortable. The Bible, especially those words in the New Testament written in red, are not too comfortable at some points.

Once in His home territory of Galilee, our Lord Jesus addressed this subject specifically. He called upon us to see our world through His eyes. He challenged us to look backward, outward, inward and upward. He instructed us regarding our pattern, our potential, our problem, and our priority. He called upon us to see four very important things in our text.

Our pattern...how do we discover it? ...look backward

 Then Jesus went about all the cities and villages, teaching in their synagogues, preaching the gospel of the kingdom, and healing every sickness and every disease among the people.

But when He saw the multitudes, He was moved with

compassion for them, because they were weary and scat-
tered, like sheep having no shepherd (Matt. 9:35-36).

The Lord Jesus stayed busy. He "went about all the cities and villages" (Matt. 9:35). He was out there among the people. He did not find a comfortable spot, some comfort zone, and wait for them to come to Him. The Bible tells us He was "teaching." Matthew uses a New Testament word here to describe that our Lord was instructing, explaining, expounding to the people. The tense also indicates that this was a continual thing. He stayed at it. Note he was also "preaching." Here the word means to proclaim as a herald. We can see Him as He was standing on street corners and heralding what? Seven habits of successful people? Some new phrase of popular psychology? Five ways to possibility thinking? No. The text tells us He was preaching the "gospel." He was laying forth the good news. Then, He was "healing." The Greek word here is therapeurō. It means to cure and one can readily see that we get our English word therapeutic from this Greek word. It is important to see that the Lord Jesus was not only teaching and preaching but He was touching physical, mental and emotional needs. He was with the hurting. He got down where they were. There was something therapeutic about His very presence.

This is our pattern for ministry. We look back to Him to find it. It has to do with the head. He was teaching. It has to do with the heart. He was preaching. It has to do with the hand. He was healing, He was touching people's needs. Some of us gravitate to one or the other and get out of balance in the process. Some have only preaching with a strong emphasis on evangelism. Others are overbalanced on teaching. They fill minds with truth but make little application. Some others are busy getting their hands dirty with social action but with little mention of evangelism or teaching. Our Lord Jesus Christ was balanced in his approach. He is our pattern for ministry. Our Lord didn't stay within His little group of twelve. There were important times for that, but by and large He was "out there" among the people in the villages and cities.

Then something happened. "But when He saw the multitudes, He was moved with compassion for them" (Matt. 9:36). While others looked, Jesus saw. There's a difference between looking and seeing. The word we find here is translated in most other passages and scripture as "to know or to perceive." Jesus saw right into their hearts and He knew them. Have we seen the multitudes lately? Oh, we're not asking ourselves if we've looked at them. Have we seen them? Do we know what they're thinking? Do we know how they're hurting? Some of us drive past a hundred mission opportunities to come to our churches and pray for our missionaries in faraway lands. Jesus "saw" the multitudes who were all around Him.

Then the Bible tells us He was "moved with compassion." The middle voice indicating that the subject was acting upon itself expresses what was deep within His innermost being. This is the motivation to get out of our comfort zones. It does not come from outside encouragement but it comes from inside of us. We remember that the good Samaritan on the Jericho road met the wounded man's need because first of all his "heart went out to him."

The Lord Jesus sees the multitudes today and He is still

moved with compassion. Why? Because they're "weary." The word means they are faint, they are about to faint, they're weakened, they're exhausted, they're about to collapse. The Lord Jesus saw them weighted down by life. Some of them were weighted down by sin, and others by circumstances like so many people today. He also saw that they were "scattered." The word means cast down or thrown down. In fact, the same word appears in Acts 27:29 to describe the anchor that was cast from the boat. It is also used in Luke 17:2 to describe the millstone tied around someone's neck and cast into the sea till it sank. It is a strong descriptive word. Jesus saw a people who had no hope. They were beaten down by the circumstances of life and sinking in their own experience. They were weary and scattered. What an apt description of so many in our world today.

Jesus goes on to say that they were "like sheep without a shepherd" (Matt. 9:36). There was no one to feed them. There was no one to lead them. They were looking for someone to point the direction to bring them provision and protection.

As we look around at our cities, do we see the same thing Jesus saw in His day? There are men and women all around us in the same circumstance and situation. They are weary and scattered like sheep having no shepherd. Oh, that more of us could see the multitude through the eyes of the Lord Jesus Christ. When we do we would see a world and we would be moved with compassion to leave our comfort zones and get involved.

Where is our pattern? We find it by looking backward to see the life of our Lord. He was busy like so many of us today. But, He saw something. Perhaps some of us have been looking and really not seeing. The Lord Jesus is our pattern. We will never get out of a comfort zone unless we become motivated from within. He calls us today to not only look backward and see our pattern, but also He reminds us of:

Our potential...how do we discover it? ...look outward

 "Then He said to His disciples the harvest truly is plentiful" (Matt. 9:37A).

Listen to our Lord. He is reminding us that we exist for those who are not here yet. He says the harvest truly is plentiful. When read in the language of the New Testament, we find no verbs here. We hear Him simply saying "harvest plentiful!" The harvest is mentioned three times in this context. This is Christ's emphasis. He is not talking about plowing nor planting nor cultivating. He is talking about the harvest! He was speaking about those in verse 36 who were weary and scattered. He said, "I came to seek and to save that which was lost" (Luke 19:10). Our Lord told His three most familiar stories in Luke 15 and the major emphasis upon each one of them was the fact that people were lost. We will never see the multitudes through the eyes of Christ until we see them as lost.

In our current church culture today it is not popular to call men and women "lost". We have other names for them today. We call them unreached or unchurched or some of us even refer to them as seekers. We refer to them as anything but lost. Thus, if we do not believe that people are truly lost, we lose the urgency to see them what? Saved! Lost. That is indeed a haunting word. That is the word that robbed heaven of its pearl of great price. That is the very word that caused the angels to bow low when He laid down His glory. That is the very word that caused the Father to turn away when His Son hung on the cross and darkness enveloped the earth. What is the real problem in our Western world today? We point to drugs, the loss of character and integrity, and a thousand other things. But the real problem is that men and women are lost, without hope and without Christ.

Jesus says, "The harvest truly is plentiful." Once in Samaria He reminded His followers to not say that there were four months into the harvest but He challenged them to lift up their eyes and look upon the fields for they were "white already under harvest." (John 4:35). Our first pastorate was in the wheat farming community of Hobart, Oklahoma on the southwestern plains. I was 24-years-old, fresh out of seminary, and I learned so much from those good and godly wheat farmers like Mervin Greb, Kenneth Lawford, John Cokely, and a host of others. They taught me about the harvest. In fact, my wife Susie and I moved to Hobart during the wheat harvest of 1972. The land is so flat there that people often say you can stand on a brick and see both oceans. You could drive as far as you could and see miles and miles of waves of wheat. They were golden at harvest. It reminded me of the patriotic anthem that exclaims, "Oh beautiful for spacious skies, for amber waves of grain." And yet, Jesus said the fields are "white unto harvest." For a young preacher this was confusing. What I saw were amber, golden grains of wheat when it was time for harvest. One day I asked Mervin Greb about the harvest. He said, "Preacher, when the harvest gets white it's almost too late to harvest it. It's almost over-ripe. It means you have to get it out in a hurry when it's white. There's an urgency about it." Our Lord Jesus said the harvest is plenteous but it's also white. Men and women are ready but the time is short. It takes months to grow a good crop but harvest time is short, very short. When the time comes, the harvest must be gotten out in a hurry.

I used to sit at the old A&B Cafe off the city square in Hobart and talk to those farmers in the early morning hours. They would sit leisurely and tell their stories into the morning. However, when harvest time came they didn't sit around. They didn't sit at the tables and talk about how to run their combines or how to transport their wheat to the silos. They did not get into their pickups and drive by the fields and talk about how plenteous the crops appeared. No, the time was short. They stopped talking and got into the fields. They got their hands dirty. If they didn't get the harvest out they would lose it. How much of the harvest in America have we lost? Sometimes we find ourselves only talking about it. The heart of the Lord Jesus is on the harvest of souls right now. He wants us to see our potential and the only way we can do that is by looking outward at the fields that are ripe unto harvest.

Pastoring in that part of the world I learned what happens to wheat if it's not harvested in time. In fact, if you go down to the A&B Cafe today, they'll tell you. It'll get over-ripe. Then it will become useless, too old, it will rot and be lost forever. It will fall to the ground and decay.

The problem in America is that we are watching the rotting of a culture. Why? We're quick to point our fingers at the legislature, the judicial branch, or the administrative branch of government. But, the harvest is plentiful, it is white unto harvest.

However, the church has not gotten into the fields. Too many of us have hunkered down within our four walls. We seem to be down at our own A&B Cafe, cozy and comfortable within our comfort zones. Our culture does not know Christ because we have left the harvest rotting and not made Him known. And all the while Jesus continues to cry, "the harvest truly is plentiful."

Some of us think we cannot harvest until we plant. Did it ever occur to us that the Lord Jesus Christ has been planting? He said one plants, another cultivates, and another reaps the harvest. He has been working on hearts. He has been plowing, He has been cultivating. Remember, He is the Lord of the harvest. He told those disciples when they were in Samaria that the fields were "white already unto harvest." But, who plowed the fields in Samaria? Who planted in Sychar? The disciples? No, they'd never even entered into the village. Those folks had never heard a gospel witness. Who plowed and planted? God did. He was working on empty hearts.

We look backward to see our pattern but we also look outward to see our potential. The harvest is plenteous. Do we see it? Jesus goes on to remind us of:

Our problem…how do we discover it? …look inward

 "The laborers are few" (Matthew 9:37b).

Things haven't changed much. The crowds still come. After all, our Lord had thousands of folks gathered on the Gallilean hillside but when it got right down to it, He only had 120 in the upper room who truly left their comfort zones. Jesus said the problem today was the problem then, "the laborers are few." Oh, not the spectators. They are many but those who truly look back and see their pattern, and look outward and see their potential, and those who leave their comfort zones are few.

God's problem today is not out there in the fields. They are plenteous. They are waiting. They are ready for harvest. Men and women in our cities are ripe to be harvested. They've tried everything else. They are weary. They are scattered. They do not know Christ paid for their sins on Calvary. They think it best that He might have made a little down payment and they have to work the rest of the way. We have good news to share with them. But when we look inward we find our real problem.

God's problem is with His own people. "The laborers are few." This must break His heart and certainly ought to break ours. When deacons have to be begged to share their faith. When Sunday School teachers wait for us to come to them instead of leaving comfort zones and getting into the harvest, it must break the heart of Christ. When we see a world in need of the Gospel and so many of us in our comfort zones, we see the reality of His exclamation, "the laborers are few."

Our Lord calls us to look backward and see our pattern, to look outward and see our potential, to look inward and see our problem, and finally, He calls upon us to see:

Our priority...how do we discover it? ...look upward

 Therefore pray the Lord of the harvest to send out laborers into His harvest (Matthew 9:38).

Here's the heart of Christ's message. If we miss this we miss all that Jesus is trying to say to us on World Missions Day. "Therefore pray!" Matthew uses a word to describe what Jesus is saying here. The word we translate "pray" means to ask or to beg. Yes, we're supposed to plead, to beg. But some of us are pleading and begging the wrong person. We think we're to plead and beg those in the church to go into the harvest fields, but note that Jesus moves prayer up to the front of the priority list for the harvest! Since the harvest is plenteous and the laborers are few, our natural inclination is to do anything we can to enlist workers. We beg them. We plead with them. We coerce them. Some of us even try to motivate them by guilt. But Jesus points to intercessory prayer as the primary resource to move men and women out of their comfort zones, to get them out there into the harvest.

The Lord Jesus always made prayer His own priority. Before choosing His first twelve laborers, the Apostles, He prayed all evening. Then He chose them and sent them into the harvest (Luke 6:12-13). He did not have to beg them nor to plead with them. He prayed and God the Father moved in their hearts and they were ready!

The Lord Jesus says, "Pray." But pray for what? Should the object of our prayer be in the direction of those in the fields? No, Jesus says we are to pray for "laborers." Some of us are busy praying for neighbors, or friends, or family members. We should be praying that God would send someone to leave their comfort zone and go to them and reap the harvest. This should be exciting to all to all of us. What would happen if we would see people as Christ sees them and pray that He would send forth laborers into the harvest? He would send some of us who were earnestly praying!

The Lord Jesus says to pray the Lord to what? He challenges us to pray that the Lord would "send out" laborers. Here we come to the place in our English text that we can never grasp the meaning of unless we read it in the language in which it was written. There are four words in Greek which we translate "send" in our New Testament. What was Jesus saying? Was He using the word that's translated "send" in Acts 13:3 when he says that the church at Antioch sent out Paul and Silas? The word there means to "release, or to let go." Was He using this stronger in Acts 13:4 when He said the Holy Spirit "sent" Barnabas and Saul on their missionary journey? Here the word is prefaced with a strong preposition meaning that the Holy Spirit thrust them out. Did He perhaps use the word that we find in Matthew 10 verse 5 when the word translated means to "send with an official summons"? We get our word "apostle" from that word. None of these words were used in our text. The word here is ekballō. It means to throw out with a violent motion. The same word is translated in Matthew 21:12 when Jesus threw out the money changers from the temple area. The same word is used in Acts 27:38 during the shipwreck when the sailors were busy "throwing out the cargo."

Jesus is saying that we are to pray to the Lord of the harvest that He will pick up and thrust out people into His harvest fields. That men and women can literally do no other. How much better when He sends us? The Lord Jesus didn't tell the disciples to go out and recruit workers but to pray that the Lord would so move on their hearts that they could do no other. Fresh on my mind as I pen these words were those days in my life when I was being called into the ministry. There was simply no option! I knew God had picked me up and thrust me out into His harvest.

It's interesting to note that our Lord is not just sending us into the fields but into the harvest. This is the pressing need today. That is, the harvest. It is already ripe. Our Lord sees it. Do we? And, it is important to note that He is the Lord of the harvest. Consequently, whose harvest is it? It is His harvest. What a privilege for us to be a part of the harvest.

The time is ripe for us to leave our comfort zones. These words from our Lord are a challenge to look backward. The Lord Jesus is our pattern. He left His own comfort zone and found Himself out there among the people who were in need. This is also a challenge to look outward. This is our potential. The harvest is all around us. This is also a challenge for us to look inward. This is really our problem. Do we see it? The laborers are few! Finally, our Lord's challenge is one to look upward. This should be our priority. To call upon Him. To ask Him to send out laborers into His harvest field.

Our Lord Jesus left his own comfort zone because you were part of the harvest. He laid aside His glory. He worked upon you and me through circumstances, perhaps through suffering, perhaps a word fitly spoken like apples of gold and settings of silver. Perhaps some of us are weary. Others of us may feel scattered. He sees us and His heart is still moved with compassion for us.

> *Hark the voice of Jesus calling*
> *Who will come and work for me*
> *Fields are white and harvest waiting*

Who will bear the sheaths away
Loud and long the Master calleth
Rich reward He offers free
Who will answer gladly saying
Here am I send me, send me!

"Hark the Voice of Jesus Calling"
Words by Daniel March

Christmas Day:
Let us now go to Bethlehem

Luke 2:15

It was an amazing night. Frederick Speakman, in his book *The Salty Tang*, put it like this, "It was silent and yet there was music. It was dark and yet there was light." Bethlehem almost missed it. No room! Many of us recall the moment of the birth of our first born. The trip to the hospital, the sterile environment, the presence of family and friends. But on the first Christmas a young pregnant Jewess found herself without the decency of even a clean sheet on a simple cot. In her hour of childbirth her bed was straw in a stable and when the baby was born, with trembling, yet thankful, fingers she wrapped the baby in cloths and laid him in a manger.

Down the hillside from the small village was a group of common shepherds. While the big event was transpiring unannounced in Bethlehem they had a surprise visit from heaven itself. After the angelic announcement of the Messiah's birth and the praise song of the heavenly choir, the shepherds said one to another, "Let us now go to Bethlehem and see this thing that has come to pass, which the Lord has made known to us" (Luke 2:15). And they came. And they found Him. Then they "returned glorifying and praising God for all the things they had heard and seen, as it was told them." (Luke 2:20).

Nestled on the top of a Judean mountain about six miles south of Jerusalem, Bethlehem has had a long and memorable history. It is first mentioned in scripture when Rachel died there and her heartbroken husband Jacob buried her just outside the city (Gen. 35:19). It was Bethlehem where Ruth, the Moabitess, fell in love with Boaz, the Lord of the harvest (Ruth 1:22). It was in this same village that David as a boy tended the sheep of his father and where he was anointed king by the prophet Samuel (I Sam. 17:15). It was Bethlehem, centuries before the coming of Christ, that Micah foretold would be the birthplace of the coming Messiah (Mic. 5:2).

As we walk through Bethlehem today it is still a small village on the side of the same hill. Fifty thousand residents call this town on Israel's Palestinian-controlled West Bank their home. Their tiny streets are invaded by over one million visitors each year. Each of these pilgrims is there to visit the cave which rests underneath a large Byzantine Greek Orthodox church which has stood since 530 A.D. and itself was built over the site of the structure built by Helena, Constantine's mother, in about 325 A.D. Today Bethlehem is a troubled village, awaiting like every other city in the world the coming of the Prince of Peace. Our Lord was born into an environment in Bethlehem much like the one that prevails today. Both the Jews of Jesus' day and the Palestinians of modern times are subservient to the economic interests of their richer and more powerful neighbors. Both were in refugee camps or small villages alongside a culture that was more modern and influential. Both were victims of disgust and discrimination. And, both groups had an element within them that was prone to calling for armed revolt and violence. It was into this environment that our Lord entered our world.

Let's go to Bethlehem and while there ask ourselves a question — is my life a Bethlehem? What do we mean? Bethlehem is a place of potential. It is a place of providence. It is a place of privilege. Our Lord longs for each of us to become a Bethlehem in our own right. That is, a person of potential, providence and privilege.

Bethlehem is a place of potential

Think of it. Of all the places for Messiah to be born, God chose Bethlehem. In the words of Micah it was "little among the thousands of Judah" (Mic. 5:2). One certainly would have expected Messiah to be born in Jerusalem or at least any of the scores of towns in the region larger and more prominent than Bethlehem. But God has a way of dwelling among the lowly. He said, "I dwell in the high and holy place, but with him who has a contrite and humble spirit" (Is. 57:15). Bethlehem reminds us that the small shall be great and the last shall be first, that God brings strength from weakness and brings the base things of the world to value and to nothing the things that are valued. Yes, Bethlehem is a place of potential. Perhaps you feel insignificant, little among those around you. You, like

Bethlehem are just the person God can use. Bethlehem is a place of potential…and so are you! It may be that, like Bethlehem, you simply have not awakened to it yet.

As God looks upon us today He doesn't see us for what we are but for what we could become, if and when we make room for Him. Do you remember Simon Peter's first encounter with the Lord Jesus Christ? The Lord looked at him and saw him not for who and what he was, but for who and what he had the potential to become. He said, "You are Simon (a small pebble) but you shall be called Cephas (a rock)" (John 1:42). Jesus saw the potential that was in his life. Three and a half years later, Peter reached that potential and became the undisputed leader of the Jerusalem church.

As the Lord looks into your life and my life He sees us not for what we are now, but for what we could become. That is part of the message of Bethlehem. It is a place of potential. It was "little among the villages of Judah" (Mic. 5:2) but what potential it held. Is your life a Bethlehem, a place of potential?

God did not come to Caesar's palace to be born, nor to Herod's court. But very quietly, almost unannounced and somewhat incognito, He arrived in a seemingly insignificant little town, but a place of tremendous potential.

God is reminding us today that, even though we may seem somewhat insignificant in the eyes of the world, in His eyes we have potential for greatness. Bethlehem is a place of potential. See yourself as a Bethlehem today. You, too, are a person of potential.

Bethlehem is a place of providence

Long centuries before Christ's birth, God foretold through His prophets that Bethlehem would be the birthplace of the promised Messiah of Israel. When reports spread of the "birth of a king," Herod asked the chief priest the location of the King Messiah's prophesied birthplace. He quickly replied, "in Bethlehem of Judea"(Matt. 2:5-6). But how could this be, since Mary and Joseph lived in Nazareth, 70 miles and several days journey to the north? Bethlehem is not simply a place of potential, it is also a place of providence. God still works in the affairs of men by His own design and sovereign will.

Luke begins the story of the Christmas narrative by saying, "And it came to pass in those days that a decree went out from Caesar Augustus that all the world should be registered" (Luke 2:1). But in reality there is so much more behind that verse. The decree was not issued by Caesar but by God Himself! It was divine providence moving Caesar to issue that decree. Caesar was but a pawn in the hand of God. If there was ever a place of providence it was Bethlehem. God put the whole world in motion to fulfill His word. At just the right time He used a Roman decree to move Mary and Joseph from Nazareth to Bethlehem.

God is still at work in our world today. Daniel reminds us that "the Most High rules in the kingdoms of men" (Dan. 4:17). Solomon says, "The King's heart is in the hand of the Lord" (Prov. 21:1). God is moving behind the scenes in world affairs today. He is putting the whole world in motion to fulfill His word. There is tremendous euphoria over the unification of the European community especially in light of its common currency.

Could it be that behind it all is the hand of God fulfilling His word as He moves our world toward the coming of a one-world government with an electrifying ruler who will emerge to offer world peace and will be followed by the masses?

Bethlehem is a place of providence even though the Jews of the first century world could not see it. Put yourself in their place. They were oppressed by an invading government to whom they despised paying taxes. They were inconvenienced and incurred unexpected expenses in order to travel to Bethlehem to register for the Roman tax. They must have wondered, "Where is God?" And all the while it was the hand of God's providence behind the whole affair in order to get them to Bethlehem.

The same is true for us. Many things which may appear on the surface as problems may be nothing short of the hand of God getting us to our own Bethlehem. Perhaps you feel as inconvenienced as Mary must have felt. Talk about inconvenience, Mary had to journey 70 miles on the back of a donkey over the most rugged terrain imaginable while in her final trimester of pregnancy. And all the while God is moving behind the scenes, orchestrating by His providence your situation or circumstance and even allowing certain things to take place that do not appear to be of benefit to you. Why? In order to get you to Bethlehem so that you might see your potential and His providence. Is your life a Bethlehem?

Bethlehem reminds us that God fulfills His word. What He promises He performs no matter how insurmountable the obstacles may seem to be. If you begin to doubt some of the promises He has made to you, simply remember Bethlehem. It is a place of providence as well as potential.

Bethlehem is a place of privilege

What an awesome privilege to be the hand-picked city to cradle the Son of God. Out of all the cities in the world, why Bethlehem? Why not Jerusalem? It was the seat of religious power. But God was sending a message. The hope of the world is not in religion. Why not Rome? It was the center of political power. God wants everyone to know that the hope of the world is not in politics. What about Athens? It was the center of intellectual power. But the hope of the world is not in philosophy. God privileged the little town of Bethlehem because the hope of the world is in a Savior! Bethlehem is a place of privilege.

The Lord Jesus came on mission to Bethlehem and 33 years later that mission led Him to a cross outside the city walls of Jerusalem. But before the cross was a cradle and that cradle was divinely placed in the town of Bethlehem. But when the moment came, most of the village missed it. Divine moments come and go. How are you going to recognize them? Speakman says, "So often they show up like any other moment and so often when we are so occupied or so convinced something else we are doing is so important." And the danger is we let the moment go and never know what could have become of it, much like the Bethlehem innkeeper.

This very chapter could be a Bethlehem moment for you! Like Bethlehem you too could awaken to a brand new world. The same Christ born in Bethlehem could be born again in you. Paul puts it this way, "My little children for whom I labor in birth again until Christ is formed in you" (Gal. 4:19). If we think Bethlehem is privileged to be the birthplace of our Lord, what a greater privilege for Him to be born in us. When much of our world has never even heard His sweet name what a privilege for Him to reside in us.

In my library I have an old antique book written by a man named Phillips Brooks. He was pastor of Holy Trinity Church in Philadelphia in the nineteenth century. In 1865 he made a personal pilgrimage to the Holy Land. Unlike the one I made recently, it took Brooks several weeks on board ship instead of several hours on board a jumbo jet. On Christmas Eve he made his way from Jerusalem to Bethlehem by horseback. The scene and experience were forever etched in his mind. Back home in Philadelphia during the Christmas season of 1868 his mind was flooded with memories of the earlier Bethlehem Christmas. He sat at his desk and the words began to flow from his pen to the paper. He penned the words that night that we believers have sung for over a century now known as "O Little Town of Bethlehem." Thinking of Bethlehem, Phillips Brooks put it this way — "the hopes and fears of all the years are met in thee tonight." Yes, the hopes and fears of all the years were met in Bethlehem that night. Christina Rosetti put "that night" in the following poetic language:

> *That night when shepherds heard the song of angelic hosts caroling near,*

> *A deaf man turned in slumbers spell and dreamed that he could hear.*

> *That night when in the cattle stall slept mother and child in humble fold,*

A cripple turned his twisted limbs and dreamed that he was whole.

That night when o'er the new born babe a tender mother rose to lean,

A loathsome leper smiled in sleep and dreamed that he was clean.

That night when to the mother's breast the little king was held secure,

A harlot slept a happy sleep and dreamed she was pure.

That night when in the manger lay the Holy One who came to save,

A man turned in the sleep of death and dreamed there was no grave.

What shall be our gift to him?

What shall I give him poor as I am?

If I were a shepherd I'd give him a lamb.

If I were a wise man I'd do my part.

What shall I give him?

I know…I'll give him my heart!

And when we do, we too, become a Bethlehem, a place of potential, providence, and privilege.